Selections from

SWINBURNE

Selections from SWINBURNE

EDITED
BY
H. M. BURTON

CAMBRIDGE
AT THE UNIVERSITY PRESS
1927

CAMBRIDGE
UNIVERSITY PRESS

University Printing House, Cambridge CB2 8BS, United Kingdom

Published in the United States of America by Cambridge University Press, New York

Cambridge University Press is part of the University of Cambridge.

It furthers the University's mission by disseminating knowledge in the pursuit of education, learning and research at the highest international levels of excellence.

www.cambridge.org
Information on this title: www.cambridge.org/9781107681620

First published 1927
First paperback edition 2014

A catalogue record for this publication is available from the British Library

ISBN 978-1-107-68162-0 Paperback

PREFACE

There are a number of reasons, many of them excellent, why Swinburne is not yet a 'popular' poet, not even a 'school-room' poet; it is approximately these reasons which have determined the 'make-up' of this selection. There may be critics in whom the idea of a Swinburne without "Hertha" or "Dolores," without "Tiresias" or "A Hymn to Proserpine" will arouse amusement, perhaps indignation; but in dealing with a poet whose appeal—to both heart and head—is so wide and so deep, the general virtue of selection becomes at once a particular necessity. There have, too, been considerations of space.

The editor has aimed at representing the variable and inconsistent quality of Swinburne's genius, so that while, for obvious reasons, certain splendid poems have been omitted, other poems, less memorable, have for other reasons been included. The ultimate effect, it is hoped, will be to send the reader to the full and complete Works, as published by Messrs Heinemann, by arrangement with whom the present extracts and poems are reprinted.

H. M. B.

1927

CONTENTS

* Poems or passages marked with an asterisk are not printed complete.

INTRODUCTION

There is scarcely a poet whose work presents so many problems, to the expert reader as well as to the beginner, as Algernon Charles Swinburne. Much of the difficulty arises from his great learning. At seventeen he was already deeply and widely read in the Bible, in the Classics, in Elizabethan Drama and in French and Italian literature; and as time went on he added to his learning, remembered what he had read, and ransacked history and legend for further material. Yet he was no bookworm. His life, certainly, was not crowded with action, especially during his last thirty years; but he was always a keen lover of the open air, the winds, the sea; in his youth he rode and swam and loved; he was an entertaining conversationalist and possessed to the end a youthful sense of humour and of fun. It is not solely, therefore, as a scholar that he is to be approached.

His work, again, was often derivative, but never imitative. It is not difficult to trace, here and there, the note of Rossetti, the influence of Baudelaire, perhaps even of Browning, yet he never imitated any of these. If he used the same instrument, perhaps even the same mode and the same tone, the melody he played was always distinctly and particularly his own.

He was capable, too, of astounding variations within his own limits. He would spread himself out over eight hundred lines of a "Song for the Centenary of Walter Savage Landor," or rattle off a "Marching Song" of over two hundred lines which no army could be expected to understand, if ever it could memorise it; and yet he could compress into eight lines everything that the following stanza of "Rococo" suggests:

Dream that the lips once breathless
  Might quicken if they would;
Say that the soul is deathless;
  Dream that the gods are good;
Say March may wed September,
  And time divorce regret;
But not that you remember,
  And not that I forget.

He could be convincingly pagan, as in the "Hymn to Proserpine," and as convincingly devout, as in "St. Dorothy." He could be sublime, as in "Prelude," or "Ave Atque Vale," or merely noisy (as in "March: an Ode") or commonplace (as in most of his poems on childhood). There seems no end to the contradictions; the more closely one studies Swinburne's poetry, the less certainly one feels safe from these alarms. Even his finest work will not always bear inspection; a neat antithesis catches the eye and the ear, but one discovers that, after all, the balance, in *sense*, is not so perfect; a simile is begun—usually something is being compared with the sea or the wind or the sun—and it runs on magnificently until one realises suddenly that one has forgotten—possibly the poet himself has forgotten—what originally was the subject of the comparison; again and again one notes an unnecessary passage that was suggested, or even enforced, by a word for which there exists only one rhyme in the language! Again and again, in one page, in one poem, one meets the same word, the same overworked alliteration, the same meaningless phrase—'spirit of sense' or 'sense of soul' confusing both sense *and* soul as they tumble over one another.

Yet out of this mass of contradictions, of lapses in taste and of errors in style, there arises poem after poem which, as a whole, is undeniably great, which takes away the breath not merely at the first reading, but every time. A critic has pointedly said that "the whole of Swinburne is greater than the sum of his parts."

Nor does a study of his life offer any great help in the solution of the problem. He was born in 1837, while his parents were staying in London. His father, of an ancient Border family, was an Admiral in the Navy; his mother, a charming and cultured lady, a daughter of the Earl of Ashburnham. He inherited blue blood and a love of the sea; but none of his ancestors, on either side, had ever shown literary leanings. His boyhood was spent almost entirely at his grandfather's seat in Northumberland, or at the house in the Isle of Wight where his father had settled on his retirement. By day he swam or rode fearlessly, and at night his mother would read to him or teach him Italian. At Eton he played no games and won no prizes, but he was not unpopular, and his brilliant red head, bent over a great folio in a window-seat of the College library, became one of the sights of the place. In the Dedication to *Poems and Ballads* (First Series) he claimed that some of his verses had been written at Eton, but this was almost certainly not true, since he himself declared, later in life, that he had destroyed everything he had written up to the age of eighteen.

At Oxford he created a mild sensation because of his hair and his bright clothes and his Republican views—and also, perhaps, because of certain queer mannerisms and gestures due to a form of St Vitus' Dance; but on the whole his University career was not a success. He won a Scholarship for French and Italian Literature but took no degree, and his Prize poem, on "The Discovery of the North-West Passage," was unsuccessful. It was almost certainly better than the winning poem, but it as certainly did not follow the prescribed subject. At any rate, Swinburne was deeply hurt and never again referred to Oxford, save with disgust.

He came before the public first in 1860 with two plays, neither of which caused the slightest stir; but in 1865 appeared *Atalanta in Calydon*, the most famous of his longer works, and in many ways better than anything else he ever did.

The 'argument' of the drama (taken, of course, from Greek legend), is told at the beginning in a beautiful piece of archaic prose; but the play would be quite intelligible without it. Classical scholars have said that in spirit it is not truly Hellenic, but for the average reader the poem seems like the translation of an unusually lucid Greek tragedy. The fame it brought Swinburne was immediate, and of the right sort, and the publication of *Poems and Ballads*, in 1866, although it introduced his name to a wider circle, scarcely enhanced his reputation.

Poems and Ballads created just that scandalous success which greets any vastly daring work of art and which, if the work be of inferior, or even average, merit, soon kills it. There was, undoubtedly, much that was offensive in the book, but it was neither so bad as its contemporary critics believed it, nor so great as its modern supporters would have us believe it to-day. Together with Rossetti's *Poems* (1870) it elicited the notorious article on the "Fleshly School of Poetry," by Buchanan, in which it was said of Swinburne that "the first feelings of disgust. . . faded away into comic amazement. It was only a little mad boy letting off squibs."

It was, of course, a good deal more than that, and the 'squibs' still, after over sixty years, retain much of their original sparkle and fire. It must be remembered that in 1866 English poetry had run itself into a groove of a pleasantly sentimental futility. Tennyson was Poet Laureate, and to the sadly Victorianised *Idylls of the King* had just added *Enoch Arden*, another lush and stereotyped story in verse. Browning, preparing *The Ring and the Book*, had been two years silent. Matthew Arnold had published only *Merope*, Rossetti's poems were still in manuscript, most of William Morris's yet unwritten—except the *Defence of Guinevere* which had been almost completely ignored. Coventry Patmore and Mrs Browning, leaders both of Victorian sentimentalism, were wildly popular.

It was on this peaceful and idyllic midsummer day that Swinburne's thunderclap burst, and in the chorus of disapprobation that arose there was often a note of resentment that the slumbers had been so rudely disturbed. Swinburne presented several defences. On the accusation that his verses were immoral, he would ask to be informed exactly where the immorality lay, and then naïvely retort that the explanation was far more immoral than his poem! He might equally have pleaded that his poems were no more expressions of his own beliefs than, say, King Richard III's "I am determined to prove a villain" was a confession of Shakespeare's own villainy. His "Hymn to Proserpine," for example, which was the prayer of an ancient Roman, a priest of the Old Gods, on the proclamation of the Christian Faith in Rome, was held to be profane and anti-Christian; it would have been surprisingly bad workmanship had it appeared anything but anti-Christian.

His strongest defence, however, whether he offered it sincerely or not, was that English poetry had needed a strong and alarming shock, and that he had administered that shock. His greatest error, after all, among many minor errors of taste and of style, was that he had attempted to load the sensitiveness, the licences, the sensuality of French poetry on to the English language—which was incapable of bearing them with the right grace and delicacy—for the benefit of the English public—which was totally unprepared for them.

This volume of 1866 contains features that adorned or

marred Swinburne's poetry until the end of his days. Among the adornments must be numbered his love of the sea, and his genius in referring to it. In "The Triumph of Time" there are many touching references to the 'mother and lover of men, the sea'; the "Two Dreams" contains an authentic touch:

> As sea-water, having killed over-heat
> In a man's body, chills it with faint ache,

and this note occurs again and again in his later work, sometimes coupled with the sun, often with the winds, but most often alone. "O to me," he writes in "The Garden of Cymodoce,"

> Mother more dear than love's own longing, sea,
> More than love's eyes are, fair....
> For song I have loved with second love, but thee,
> Thee first, thee, mother....

Tristram swam

> Between the live sea and the living sun,
> And mightier grew the joy to meet full-faced
> Each wave, and mount with upward plunge, and taste
> The rapture of its rolling strength, and cross
> Its flickering crown of snows that flash and toss
> Like plumes in battle's blithest charge, and thence
> To match the next with yet more strenuous sense;

while "Ex Voto" ends with

> But when my time shall be,
> O mother, O my sea,
> Alive or dead, take me,
> Me too, my mother.

Another of Swinburne's outstanding merits, so early apparent, is his genius for versification. English poetry of his day was cast into one or other of but three or four moulds, chief of which were the iambic pentameter and the more hackneyed lyric measures. *Poems and Ballads* contains about sixty poems, and over forty different metres, some of them experimental and never repeated, others to become favourites with Swinburne. This variety of metre was in itself enough to have won for the poet something better than mere howls of censure, and Swinburne's interest and achievement in versification never left him; occasionally, in fact, they ran away with him.

There appear, however, side by side with his virtues, not a few of his poetic vices. Some of them are aptly illustrated in the very passage from *Tristram of Lyonesse* quoted above (written, however, some sixteen years after 1866). At first glance "the live sea and the living sun" seems a neat and expressive line; but it is not long before one wonders precisely what difference Swinburne meant to convey between 'live' and 'living,' and why the sea should be anything but 'live,' or the sun anything but 'living.' In the last line of the passage Tristram prepares to meet the next wave with "yet more strenuous sense." It is doubtful whether 'more strenuous sense' means anything at all; at best it suggests something that would be of little enough use against a mighty wave, and it is impossible to avoid the suspicion that 'sense,' a favourite 'duty word' with Swinburne, stepped nobly into the breach as a rhyme for 'thence.'

This suspicion of 'fake,' though it occurs more often in his later work, is not entirely absent from his earlier. The last stanza of "The Garden of Proserpine," for example, contains an unlovely word, 'diurnal,' which has little significance in its context, but serves admirably, if inevitably, as a rhyme for 'vernal' and 'eternal.' Even "The Triumph of Time"—which was wrung from the poet, together with "A Leave-Taking," after his only serious love-affair had ended unhappily, and is sincere and heartfelt—even this contains its little insincerities. "I wish," he writes,

> I wish we were dead together to-day....
> Clasped and clothed in the cloven clay.

This second line, with its horrible array of alliterations which are neither beautiful nor useful, means little more than 'buried together.'

> Body for body and blood for blood,

he writes elsewhere, and is at once, as it were, 'up against it' for a rhyme to 'blood.' The temptation is too strong for this sea-mew, and back, for the sixth time in twelve stanzas, comes the sea—

> As the flow of the full sea risen to flood.

Of the forty-nine stanzas in "The Triumph of Time," moreover, quite half could easily have been omitted, with little loss in sense, and much compensatory gain in power and 'thrust.'

These criticisms may appear cavilling and ungenerous, but they need detract but little from our appreciation and enjoyment of the poems. To estimate accurately is to enjoy more completely, and a realisation of the weaknesses we have studied is essential to an accurate estimate. It is mainly these weaknesses that have led some to suppose that Swinburne is 'all sound and no sense,' which is not entirely a just criticism. Often enough there is little sense in his verse apart from the sound, but in these instances sound and sense may be inseparable, just as (to take a far cruder example than any Swinburne ever attempted) they are inseparable in Southey's *How the waters come down at Lodore*. Occasionally, it is true, the noise is so overwhelming in Swinburne as completely to drown the ideas, and sometimes, unfortunately, there is neither sound nor sense worth mention. But in the face of *Atalanta*, of "Ave Atque Vale," of "Prelude," and of many another masterpiece, it is ridiculous to dismiss Swinburne's work as merely 'sound and fury, signifying nothing.'

Poems and Ballads was followed by volume after volume.

If there was any doubt as to quality there was never any as to quantity. *Songs before Sunrise* (1871) was partly the result of an almost amusing little plot by his friends. Here was a young man of infinite possibilities, wasting his genius, it seemed, over little lusts and petty legends. "What," they said in effect, "is to be done with our Algernon?" Mazzini, the Prophet of Italian liberation, was in England, an exile; it was known that Swinburne worshipped Liberty in the abstract, and Mazzini in particular; the rest was easy. The two great men were introduced. Swinburne fell at Mazzini's feet and more or less promised to devote his energies to Italy. He had scarcely seen Italy—never seen, at any rate, the results of Austrian misrule, the "negation of God erected into a principle," as Gladstone had seen them at Naples. He ignored the fact (presumably he knew it) that Mazzini's share in Italian liberation was only a part, and that not the greatest part, and futile without the work of Cavour, of Garibaldi, and of others. His passion for liberty was entirely academic—he neither fought, like Byron, in the cause, nor went into exile, like Shelley—even though it was magnificent.

The result may almost be imagined. The poet in him would not be gainsaid, and *Songs before Sunrise* contained much fine work, some, indeed, like "Hertha," "The Pilgrims," "Tiresias," his very finest work in a certain strain —the philosophical; but it contained, also, much sound and fury, "a whirlwind in a vacuum," top-heavy songs and endless odes. *Songs of Two Nations*, which followed, and was in the same strain, was even worse, and the poet's star began to wane.

Meanwhile his health, too, was waning. He was never a mere drunkard, but his friends were not of the wisest, and his habits were indiscreet. He was subject to most distressing fits, as well as to complete collapses. Again and again his father would be summoned to London and would carry Algernon off to the country, whence, amazingly recovered, the poet would return to the whirl of London for another spell. Eventually he was rescued from his troubles, both physical and financial, and carried off to Putney by Theodore Watts (afterwards Watts-Dunton) with whom he lived for the last thirty years of his life.

It may be true, as many have argued, that Watts-Dunton clipped the brilliant wings and kept the splendid falcon closely hooded. It may be true, equally, that he influenced his judgments, led him away from the gaieties and spontaneities of youth to the sober respectability of suburban middle-age, that he persuaded Swinburne to bow down to the Watts-Dunton idols and to revile his own. But it is just as true that he nursed Swinburne back to health and kept him there, that he encouraged his brilliant and scholarly researches into Elizabethan literature, and that he managed his affairs as Swinburne himself never could have begun to manage them. From No. 2, The Pines, Putney Hill, Swinburne published many volumes of prose and verse, much of them definitely bad, some readable, but unworthy of their author, a small body (including *The Tale of Balen* among other things) almost as fine as his best.

Deafness came with advancing age and restricted his opportunities for social intercourse, but he remained a courtly, kind, sprightly little gentleman, his red hair a little dulled, his step no less jerky and nervous, a familiar figure in the neighbourhood on his daily walks up Putney Hill and over Wimbledon Common. He died, in 1909, of pneumonia.

Beside the great volume of his verse he wrote several dramas and a considerable body of prose criticism. The Dramas contain much fine poetry and some exquisite songs, but Swinburne never realised that speeches of a hundred lines or so, even when accurately memorised, are apt to become a trifle dull on the stage. His plays are nearly all too long. He is said once to have thrown himself suddenly at the feet of Jowett, Master of Balliol, and exclaimed, "Master! I have never thanked you enough for cutting *four thousand* lines out of *Bothwell*!"

His prose is at times sublime, and, like his verse, at times ridiculous. As a critic, he will live for his study of William Blake (the last and greatest word on the subject) and for his essay on Shakespeare. But he was wont to be so prodigal of his praise that he would find himself without a single shot in his locker when the critical moment for praise actually arrived; and, on the other hand, to spoil the effect of his censure by furious passages of contumely and execration. He also, unfortunately, allowed himself to be persuaded, in his later years, to recant the praises of his youth and to dole out obloquy on his earlier idols.

To sum him up is no easy task, where there is so much that is sterling to be offset by so much that is dross. Several critics have emphasised his weakness of 'outline'; despite his knowledge and love of the Greek Classics he seemed unable to envisage a poem as a whole, and to write it with an eye on the general shape and design of the completed work, as distinguished from the perfection of the detail. It is certain that he was no descriptive poet; he seldom described, seldom even seemed to see, anything deeper than the most obvious features and phenomena of Nature. Even his beloved sea is seldom actually described, and, except in a rhapsodic, intoxicated way, he was no real lover of Nature. His inspiration came nearly always from within; occasionally an incident or an event would provide an immediate cause for a poem, but the cause would be little more than a peg on which to hang the richly woven fabric of his own dreams and thoughts. As often as his poetry appears to be inspired by something external, something outside his own heart and brain, so often does it tend to sink towards the commonplace.

A recent writer has maintained that Swinburne was strangely insensible to any influences that he encountered after his youth. The main currents in his poetry are his obsession with the elements, with Northumberland, with the Classics, with Elizabethan Drama, with medievalism, with liberty and with childhood; his hero-worship of Victor Hugo, of Landor, of Villon, of Baudelaire, of Sappho, of Mazzini; and his exquisite gift for versification. For every one of these 'causes,' great or little (with the exception of childhood) he is known to have conceived a passion either at Eton or at Oxford. In after life he merely enlarged or intensified his obsessions; he exhausted every vein in his mines, one by one, and tapped no new ones.

As an indication of this insensibility to outside influences it is interesting to note that he knew little of, and cared less for, the work of any poet born after about 1850. Of his contemporaries he knew and loved Rossetti best of all. When Rossetti, in his grief at the death of his young wife, buried the manuscript of all his poems in the coffin with her, Swinburne was able to dictate them almost word-perfectly from memory; and when, years later, the poems were 'disinterred,' it was found that Swinburne had made few mistakes, and those unimportant.

He founded no school, but he left an unmistakable mark on our poetic literature. He found it stereotyped and formal; he left it plastic and infinitely variable. On the dull and decent background of Victorian modesty he imposed a brilliant and kaleidoscopic network of colour and design. English poetry is still mainly lyrical, still singing in the tones and accents he taught it, and it is only the dead-weight of so much dross in his work, the mass, too, of his own erudition, that have prevented his becoming more than a 'poet's poet.' His work made possible a fuller appreciation of Tennyson as well as of Browning, and without him much of Rossetti and Morris would seem incomplete and 'unbuttoned.'

His style lends itself to parody, but not, since it is so individual, to imitation. Two quotations may well serve as last words on this contradictory poet. One is by Coventry Patmore, a contemporary whom he pitilessly parodied: "It is impossible not to feel that there has been some disproportion between his power of saying things and the things he has to say." The other is a stanza or two from one of the finest parodies in the language, *The Octopus*, by A. C. Hilton (1851–1877):

O breast, that 'twere rapture to writhe on!
  O arms 'twere delicious to feel
Clinging close with the crush of the Python,
  When she maketh her murderous meal!
In thy eight-fold embraces enfolden,
  Let our empty existence escape;
Give us death that is glorious and golden,
  Crushed all out of shape!

Ah! thy red lips, lascivious and luscious,
  With death in their amorous kiss,
Cling round us, and clasp us, and crush us,
  With bitings of agonised bliss;
We are sick with the poison of pleasure,
  Dispense us the potion of pain;
Ope thy mouth to its uttermost measure
  And bite us again!

Lines like these contained, apart from their mere good spirits, a truer estimate and a more valuable criticism, than all the fulminations of Swinburne's shocked contemporaries.

The Triumph of Time

We had stood as the sure stars stand, and moved
As the moon moves, loving the world; and seen
Grief collapse as a thing disproved,
Death consume as a thing unclean.
Twain halves of a perfect heart, made fast
Soul to soul while the years fell past;
Had you loved me once, as you have not loved;
Had the chance been with us that has not been.

I have put my days and dreams out of mind,
Days that are over, dreams that are done.
Though we seek life through, we shall surely find
There is none of them clear to us now, not one.
But clear are these things; the grass and the sand,
Where, sure as the eyes reach, ever at hand,
With lips wide open and face burnt blind,
The strong sea-daisies feast on the sun.

The low downs lean to the sea; the stream,
One loose thin pulseless tremulous vein,
Rapid and vivid and dumb as a dream,
Works downward, sick of the sun and the rain;
No wind is rough with the rank rare flowers;
The sweet sea, mother of loves and hours,
Shudders and shines as the grey winds gleam,
Turning her smile to a fugitive pain.

Mother of loves that are swift to fade,
Mother of mutable winds and hours.
A barren mother, a mother-maid,
Cold and clean as her faint salt flowers.

I would we twain were even as she,
Lost in the night and the light of the sea,
Where faint sounds falter and wan beams wade,
  Break, and are broken, and shed into showers.

* * * * * *

It is not much that a man can save
  On the sands of life, in the straits of time,
Who swims in sight of the great third wave
  That never a swimmer shall cross or climb.
Some waif washed up with the strays and spars
That ebb-tide shows to the shore and the stars;
Weed from the water, grass from a grave,
  A broken blossom, a ruined rhyme.

There will no man do for your sake, I think,
  What I would have done for the least word said.
I had wrung life dry for your lips to drink,
  Broken it up for your daily bread:
Body for body and blood for blood,
As the flow of the full sea risen to flood
That yearns and trembles before it sink,
  I had given, and lain down for you, glad and dead.

* * * * * *

You have chosen and clung to the chance they sent you,
  Life sweet as perfume and pure as prayer.
But will it not one day in heaven repent you?
  Will they solace you wholly, the days that were?
Will you lift up your eyes between sadness and bliss,
Meet mine, and see where the great love is,
And tremble and turn and be changed? Content you;
  The gate is strait; I shall not be there.

But you, had you chosen, had you stretched hand,
  Had you seen good such a thing were done,
I too might have stood with the souls that stand
  In the sun's sight, clothed with the light of the sun;
But who now on earth need care how I live?
Have the high gods anything left to give,
Save dust and laurels and gold and sand?
  Which gifts are goodly; but I will none.

O all fair lovers about the world,
  There is none of you, none, that shall comfort me.
My thoughts are as dead things, wrecked and whirled
  Round and round in a gulf of the sea;
And still, through the sound and the straining stream,
Through the coil and chafe, they gleam in a dream,
The bright fine lips so cruelly curled,
  And strange swift eyes where the soul sits free.

* * * * * *

I will go back to the great sweet mother,
  Mother and lover of men, the sea.
I will go down to her, I and none other,
  Close with her, kiss her and mix her with me;
Cling to her, strive with her, hold her fast:
O fair white mother, in days long past
Born without sister, born without brother,
  Set free my soul as thy soul is free.

O fair green-girdled mother of mine,
  Sea, that art clothed with the sun and the rain,
Thy sweet hard kisses are strong like wine,
  Thy large embraces are keen like pain.
Save me and hide me with all thy waves,
Find me one grave of thy thousand graves,
Those pure cold populous graves of thine
  Wrought without hand in a world without stain.

I shall sleep, and move with the moving ships,
  Change as the winds change, veer in the tide;
My lips will feast on the foam of thy lips,
  I shall rise with thy rising, with thee subside;
Sleep, and not know if she be, if she were,
Filled full with life to the eyes and hair,
As a rose is fulfilled to the roseleaf tips
  With splendid summer and perfume and pride.

This woven raiment of nights and days,
  Were it once cast off and unwound from me,
Naked and glad would I walk in thy ways,
  Alive and aware of thy ways and thee;
Clear of the whole world, hidden at home,
Clothed with the green and crowned with the foam,
A pulse of the life of thy straits and bays,
  A vein in the heart of the streams of the sea.

Fair mother, fed with the lives of men,
  Thou art subtle and cruel of heart, men say.
Thou hast taken, and shalt not render again;
  Thou art full of thy dead, and cold as they.
But death is the worst that comes of thee;
Thou art fed with our dead, O mother, O sea,
But when hast thou fed on our hearts? or when,
  Having given us love, hast thou taken away?

O tender-hearted, O perfect lover,
  Thy lips are bitter, and sweet thine heart.
The hopes that hurt and the dreams that hover,
  Shall they not vanish away and apart?
But thou, thou art sure, thou art older than earth;
Thou art strong for death and fruitful of birth;
Thy depths conceal and thy gulfs discover;
  From the first thou wert; in the end thou art.

* * * * * *

I shall go my ways, tread out my measure,
  Fill the days of my daily breath
With fugitive things not good to treasure,
  Do as the world doth, say as it saith;
But if we had loved each other—O sweet,
Had you felt, lying under the palms of your feet,
The heart of my heart, beating harder with pleasure
  To feel you tread it to dust and death—

Ah, had I not taken my life up and given
  All that life gives and the years let go,
The wine and honey, the balm and leaven,
  The dreams reared high and the hopes brought low?
Come life, come death, not a word be said;
Should I lose you living, and vex you dead?
I never shall tell you on earth; and in heaven,
  If I cry to you then, will you hear or know?

A Leave-Taking

Let us go hence, my songs; she will not hear.
Let us go hence together without fear;
Keep silence now, for singing-time is over,
And over all old things and all things dear.
She loves not you nor me as all we love her.
Yea, though we sang as angels in her ear,
    She would not hear.

Let us rise up and part; she will not know.
Let us go seaward as the great winds go,
Full of blown sand and foam; what help is here?
There is no help, for all these things are so,
And all the world is bitter as a tear.
And how these things are, though ye strove to show,
    She would not know.

Let us go home and hence; she will not weep.
We gave love many dreams and days to keep,
Flowers without scent, and fruits that would not grow,
Saying "If thou wilt, thrust in thy sickle and reap."
All is reaped now; no grass is left to mow;
And we that sowed, though all we fell on sleep,
    She would not weep.

Let us go hence and rest; she will not love.
She shall not hear us if we sing hereof,
Nor see love's ways, how sore they are and steep.
Come hence, let be, lie still; it is enough.
Love is a barren sea, bitter and deep;
And though she saw all heaven in flower above,
    She would not love.

Let us give up, go down; she will not care.
Though all the stars made gold of all the air,
And the sea moving saw before it move
One moon-flower making all the foam-flowers fair;
Though all those waves went over us, and drove
Deep down the stifling lips and drowning hair,
    She would not care.

Let us go hence, go hence; she will not see.
Sing all once more together; surely she,
She too, remembering days and words that were,
Will turn a little toward us, sighing; but we,
We are hence, we are gone, as though we had not
  been there.
Nay, and though all men seeing had pity on me,
    She would not see.

Itylus

Swallow, my sister, O sister swallow,
  How can thine heart be full of the spring?
    A thousand summers are over and dead.
What hast thou found in the spring to follow?
  What hast thou found in thine heart to sing?
    What wilt thou do when the summer is shed?

O swallow, sister, O fair swift swallow,
  Why wilt thou fly after spring to the south,
    The soft south whither thine heart is set?
Shall not the grief of the old time follow?
  Shall not the song thereof cleave to thy mouth?
    Hast thou forgotten ere I forget?

Sister, my sister, O fleet sweet swallow,
  Thy way is long to the sun and the south;
    But I, fulfilled of my heart's desire,
Shedding my song upon height, upon hollow,
  From tawny body and sweet small mouth
    Feed the heart of the night with fire.

I the nightingale all spring through,
  O swallow, sister, O changing swallow,
    All spring through till the spring be done,
Clothed with the light of the night on the dew,
  Sing, while the hours and the wild birds follow,
    Take flight and follow and find the sun.

Sister, my sister, O soft light swallow,
  Though all things feast in the spring's guest-chamber,
    How hast thou heart to be glad thereof yet?
For where thou fliest I shall not follow,
  Till life forget and death remember,
    Till thou remember and I forget.

Swallow, my sister, O singing swallow,
  I know not how thou hast heart to sing.
    Hast thou the heart? is it all past over?
Thy lord the summer is good to follow,
  And fair the feet of thy lover the spring:
    But what wilt thou say to the spring thy lover?

O swallow, sister, O fleeting swallow,
  My heart in me is a molten ember
    And over my head the waves have met.
But thou wouldst tarry or I would follow,
  Could I forget or thou remember,
    Couldst thou remember and I forget.

O sweet stray sister, O shifting swallow,
  The heart's division divideth us.
    Thy heart is light as a leaf of a tree;
But mine goes forth among sea-gulfs hollow
  To the place of the slaying of Itylus,
    The feast of Daulis, the Thracian sea.

O swallow, sister, O rapid swallow,
  I pray thee sing not a little space.
    Are not the roofs and the lintels wet?
The woven web that was plain to follow,
  The small slain body, the flowerlike face,
    Can I remember if thou forget?

O sister, sister, thy first-begotten!
  The hands that cling and the feet that follow,
    The voice of the child's blood crying yet
Who hath remembered me? who hath forgotten?
  Thou hast forgotten, O summer swallow,
    But the world shall end when I forget.

A Match

If love were what the rose is,
And I were like the leaf,
Our lives would grow together
In sad or singing weather,
Blown fields or flowerful closes,
Green pleasure or grey grief;
If love were what the rose is,
And I were like the leaf.

If I were what the words are,
And love were like the tune,
With double sound and single
Delight our lips would mingle,
With kisses glad as birds are
That get sweet rain at noon;
If I were what the words are,
And love were like the tune.

If you were life, my darling,
And I your love were death,
We'd shine and snow together
Ere March made sweet the weather
With daffodil and starling
And hours of fruitful breath;
If you were life, my darling,
And I your love were death.

If you were thrall to sorrow,
And I were page to joy,
We'd play for lives and seasons
With loving looks and treasons

And tears of night and morrow
   And laughs of maid and boy;
If you were thrall to sorrow,
   And I were page to joy.

If you were April's lady,
   And I were lord in May,
We'd throw with leaves for hours
And draw for days with flowers,
Till day like night were shady
   And night were bright like day;
If you were April's lady,
   And I were lord in May.

If you were queen of pleasure,
   And I were king of pain,
We'd hunt down love together,
Pluck out his flying-feather,
And teach his feet a measure,
   And find his mouth a rein;
If you were queen of pleasure,
   And I were king of pain.

In Memory of Walter Savage Landor

Back to the flower-town, side by side,
      The bright months bring,
New-born, the bridegroom and the bride,
      Freedom and spring.

The sweet land laughs from sea to sea,
      Filled full of sun;
All things come back to her, being free;
      All things but one.

In many a tender wheaten plot
Flowers that were dead
Live, and old suns revive; but not
That holier head.

By this white wandering waste of sea,
Far north, I hear
One face shall never turn to me
As once this year:

Shall never smile and turn and rest
On mine as there,
Nor one most sacred hand be prest
Upon my hair.

I came as one whose thoughts half linger,
Half run before;
The youngest to the oldest singer
That England bore.

I found him whom I shall not find
Till all grief end,
In holiest age our mightiest mind,
Father and friend.

But thou, if anything endure,
If hope there be,
O spirit that man's life left pure,
Man's death set free,

Not with disdain of days that were
Look earthward now;
Let dreams revive the reverend hair,
The imperial brow;

Come back in sleep, for in the life
Where thou art not
We find none like thee. Time and strife
And the world's lot

Move thee no more; but love at least
And reverent heart
May move thee, royal and released,
Soul, as thou art.

And thou, his Florence, to thy trust
Receive and keep,
Keep safe his dedicated dust,
His sacred sleep.

So shall thy lovers, come from far,
Mix with thy name
As morning-star with evening-star
His faultless fame.

The Garden of Proserpine

Here, where the world is quiet;
Here, where all trouble seems
Dead winds' and spent waves' riot
In doubtful dreams of dreams;
I watch the green field growing
For reaping folk and sowing,
For harvest-time and mowing,
A sleepy world of streams.

I am tired of tears and laughter,
And men that laugh and weep;
Of what may come hereafter
For men that sow to reap:

I am weary of days and hours,
Blown buds of barren flowers,
Desires and dreams and powers
  And everything but sleep.

Here life has death for neighbour,
  And far from eye or ear
Wan waves and wet winds labour,
  Weak ships and spirits steer;
They drive adrift, and whither
They wot not who make thither;
But no such winds blow hither,
  And no such things grow here.

No growth of moor or coppice,
  No heather-flower or vine,
But bloomless buds of poppies,
  Green grapes of Proserpine,
Pale beds of blowing rushes
Where no leaf blooms or blushes
Save this whereout she crushes
  For dead men deadly wine.

Pale, without name or number,
  In fruitless fields of corn,
They bow themselves and slumber
  All night till light is born;
And like a soul belated,
In hell and heaven unmated,
By cloud and mist abated
  Comes out of darkness morn.

Though one were strong as seven,
  He too with death shall dwell,
Nor wake with wings in heaven,
  Nor weep for pains in hell;

Though one were fair as roses,
His beauty clouds and closes;
And well though love reposes,
In the end it is not well.

Pale, beyond porch and portal,
Crowned with calm leaves, she stands
Who gathers all things mortal
With cold immortal hands;
Her languid lips are sweeter
Than love's who fears to greet her
To men that mix and meet her
From many times and lands.

She waits for each and other,
She waits for all men born;
Forgets the earth her mother,
The life of fruits and corn;
And spring and seed and swallow
Take wing for her and follow
Where summer song rings hollow
And flowers are put to scorn.

There go the loves that wither,
The old loves with wearier wings;
And all dead years draw thither,
And all disastrous things;
Dead dreams of days forsaken,
Blind buds that snows have shaken,
Wild leaves that winds have taken,
Red strays of ruined springs.

We are not sure of sorrow,
And joy was never sure;
To-day will die to-morrow;
Time stoops to no man's lure;

And love, grown faint and fretful,
With lips but half regretful
Sighs, and with eyes forgetful
  Weeps that no loves endure.

From too much love of living,
  From hope and fear set free,
We thank with brief thanksgiving
  Whatever gods may be
That no life lives for ever;
That dead men rise up never;
That even the weariest river
  Winds somewhere safe to sea.

Then star nor sun shall waken,
  Nor any change of light:
Nor sound of waters shaken,
  Nor any sound or sight:
Nor wintry leaves nor vernal,
Nor days nor things diurnal;
Only the sleep eternal
  In an eternal night.

Dedication

1865

The sea gives her shells to the shingle,
  The earth gives her streams to the sea;
They are many, but my gift is single,
  My verses, the firstfruits of me.
Let the wind take the green and the grey leaf,
  Cast forth without fruit upon air;
Take rose-leaf and vine-leaf and bay-leaf
  Blown loose from the hair.

The night shakes them round me in legions,
  Dawn drives them before her like dreams;
Time sheds them like snows on strange regions,
  Swept shoreward on infinite streams;
Leaves pallid and sombre and ruddy,
  Dead fruits of the fugitive years;
Some stained as with wine and made bloody,
  And some as with tears.

Some scattered in seven years' traces,
  As they fell from the boy that was then;
Long left among idle green places,
  Or gathered but now among men;
On seas full of wonder and peril,
  Blown white round the capes of the north;
Or in islands where myrtles are sterile
  And loves bring not forth.

O daughters of dreams and of stories
  That life is not wearied of yet,
Faustine, Fragoletta, Dolores,
  Félise and Yolande and Juliette,
Shall I find you not still, shall I miss you,
  When sleep, that is true or that seems,
Comes back to me hopeless to kiss you,
  O daughters of dreams?

They are past as a slumber that passes,
  As the dew of a dawn of old time;
More frail than the shadows on glasses,
  More fleet than a wave or a rhyme.
As the waves after ebb drawing seaward,
  When their hollows are full of the night,
So the birds that flew singing to me-ward
  Recede out of sight.

The songs of dead seasons, that wander
  On wings of articulate words;
Lost leaves that the shore-wind may squander,
  Light flocks of untameable birds;
Some sang to me dreaming in class-time
  And truant in hand as in tongue;
For the youngest were born of boy's pastime,
  The eldest are young.

Is there shelter while life in them lingers,
  Is there hearing for songs that recede,
Tunes touched from a harp with man's fingers
  Or blown with boy's mouth in a reed?
Is there place in the land of your labour,
  Is there room in your world of delight,
Where change has not sorrow for neighbour
  And day has not night?

In their wings though the sea-wind yet quivers,
  Will you spare not a space for them there
Made green with the running of rivers
  And gracious with temperate air;
In the fields and the turreted cities,
  That cover from sunshine and rain
Fair passions and bountiful pities
  And loves without stain?

In a land of clear colours and stories,
  In a region of shadowless hours,
Where earth has a garment of glories
  And a murmur of musical flowers;
In woods where the spring half uncovers
  The flush of her amorous face,
By the waters that listen for lovers,
  For these is there place?

For the song-birds of sorrow, that muffle
Their music as clouds do their fire:
For the storm-birds of passion, that ruffle
Wild wings in a wind of desire;
In the stream of the storm as it settles
Blown seaward, borne far from the sun,
Shaken loose on the darkness like petals
Dropt one after one?

Though the world of your hands be more gracious
And lovelier in lordship of things
Clothed round by sweet art with the spacious
Warm heaven of her imminent wings,
Let them enter, unfledged and nigh fainting,
For the love of old loves and lost times;
And receive in your palace of painting
This revel of rhymes.

Though the seasons of man full of losses
Make empty the years full of youth,
If but one thing be constant in crosses,
Change lays not her hand upon truth;
Hopes die, and their tombs are for token
That the grief as the joy of them ends
Ere time that breaks all men has broken
The faith between friends.

Though the many lights dwindle to one light,
There is help if the heaven has one;
Though the skies be discrowned of the sunlight
And the earth dispossessed of the sun,
They have moonlight and sleep for repayment,
When, refreshed as a bride and set free,
With stars and sea-winds in her raiment,
Night sinks on the sea.

A Forsaken Garden

In a coign of the cliff between lowland and highland,
At the sea-down's edge between windward and lee,
Walled round with rocks as an inland island,
The ghost of a garden fronts the sea.
A girdle of brushwood and thorn encloses
The steep square slope of the blossomless bed
Where the weeds that grew green from the graves of its roses
Now lie dead.

The fields fall southward, abrupt and broken,
To the low last edge of the long lone land.
If a step should sound or a word be spoken,
Would a ghost not rise at the strange guest's hand?
So long have the grey bare walks lain guestless,
Through branches and briars if a man make way,
He shall find no life but the sea-wind's, restless
Night and day.

The dense hard passage is blind and stifled
That crawls by a track none turn to climb
To the strait waste place that the years have rifled
Of all but the thorns that are touched not of time.
The thorns he spares when the rose is taken;
The rocks are left when he wastes the plain.
The wind that wanders, the weeds wind-shaken,
These remain.

Not a flower to be pressed of the foot that falls not;
As the heart of a dead man the seed-plots are dry;
From the thicket of thorns whence the nightingale calls not,
Could she call, there were never a rose to reply.

Over the meadows that blossom and wither
  Rings but the note of a sea-bird's song;
Only the sun and the rain come hither
      All year long.

The sun burns sere and the rain dishevels
  One gaunt bleak blossom of scentless breath.
Only the wind here hovers and revels
  In a round where life seems barren as death.
Here there was laughing of old, there was weeping,
  Haply, of lovers none ever will know,
Whose eyes went seaward a hundred sleeping
      Years ago.

Heart handfast in heart as they stood, "Look thither,"
  Did he whisper? "look forth from the flowers to the sea;
For the foam-flowers endure when the rose-blossoms wither,
  And men that love lightly may die—but we?"
And the same wind sang and the same waves whitened,
  And or ever the garden's last petals were shed,
In the lips that had whispered, the eyes that had lightened,
      Love was dead.

Or they loved their life through, and then went whither?
  And were one to the end—but what end who knows?
Love deep as the sea as a rose must wither,
  As the rose-red seaweed that mocks the rose.
Shall the dead take thought for the dead to love them?
  What love was ever as deep as a grave?
They are loveless now as the grass above them
      Or the wave.

All are at one now, roses and lovers,
  Not known of the cliffs and the fields and the sea.
Not a breath of the time that has been hovers
  In the air now soft with a summer to be.

Not a breath shall there sweeten the seasons hereafter
Of the flowers or the lovers that laugh now or weep,
When as they that are free now of weeping and laughter
We shall sleep.

Here death may deal not again for ever;
Here change may come not till all change end.
From the graves they have made they shall rise up never,
Who have left nought living to ravage and rend.
Earth, stones, and thorns of the wild ground growing,
While the sun and the rain live, these shall be;
Till a last wind's breath upon all these blowing
Roll the sea.

Till the slow sea rise and the sheer cliff crumble,
Till terrace and meadow the deep gulfs drink,
Till the strength of the waves of the high tides humble
The fields that lessen, the rocks that shrink,
Here now in his triumph where all things falter,
Stretched out on the spoils that his own hand spread,
As a god self-slain on his own strange altar,
Death lies dead.

Ave Atque Vale

I

...It is enough; the end and the beginning
Are one thing to thee, who art past the end.
O hand unclasped of unbeholden friend,
For thee no fruits to pluck, no palms for winning,
No triumph and no labour and no lust,
Only dead yew-leaves and a little dust.

O quiet eyes wherein the light saith nought,
    Whereto the day is dumb, nor any night
    With obscure finger silences your sight,
Nor in your speech the sudden soul speaks thought,
    Sleep, and have sleep for light.

* * * * * *

II

Hast thou found any likeness for thy vision?
    O gardener of strange flowers, what bud, what bloom,
    Hast thou found sown, what gathered in the gloom?
What of despair, of rapture, of derision,
    What of life is there, what of ill or good?
    Are the fruits grey like dust or bright like blood?
Does the dim ground grow any seed of ours,
    The faint fields quicken any terrene root,
    In low lands where the sun and moon are mute
And all the stars keep silence? Are there flowers
    At all, or any fruit?

III

Alas, but though my flying song flies after,
    O sweet strange elder singer, thy more fleet
    Singing, and footprints of thy fleeter feet,
Some dim derision of mysterious laughter
    From the blind tongueless warders of the dead,
    Some gainless glimpse of Proserpine's veiled head,
Some little sound of unregarded tears
    Wept by effaced unprofitable eyes,
    And from pale mouths some cadence of dead sighs—
These only, these the hearkening spirit hears,
    Sees only such things rise.

IV

Thou art far too far for wings of words to follow,
Far too far off for thought or any prayer.
What ails us with thee, who art wind and air?
What ails us gazing where all seen is hollow?
Yet with some fancy, yet with some desire,
Dreams pursue death as winds a flying fire,
Our dreams pursue our dead and do not find.
Still, and more swift than they, the thin flame flies,
The low light fails us in elusive skies,
Still the foiled earnest ear is deaf, and blind
Are still the eluded eyes.

V

Not thee, O never thee, in all time's changes,
Not thee, but this the sound of thy sad soul,
The shadow of thy swift spirit, this shut scroll
I lay my hand on, and not death estranges
My spirit from communion of thy song—
These memories and these melodies that throng
Veiled porches of a Muse funereal—
These I salute, these touch, these clasp and fold
As though a hand were in my hand to hold,
Or through mine ears a mourning musical
Of many mourners rolled.

* * * * * *

VI

And now no sacred staff shall break in blossom,
No choral salutation lure to light
A spirit sick with perfume and sweet night
And love's tired eyes and hands and barren bosom.
There is no help for these things; none to mend
And none to mar; not all our songs, O friend,

Will make death clear or make life durable.
Howbeit with rose and ivy and wild vine
And with wild notes about this dust of thine
At least I fill the place where white dreams dwell
And wreathe an unseen shrine.

VII

Sleep; and if life was bitter to thee, pardon,
If sweet, give thanks; thou hast no more to live;
And to give thanks is good, and to forgive.
Out of the mystic and the mournful garden
Where all day through thine hands in barren braid
Wove the sick flowers of secrecy and shade,
Green buds of sorrow and sin, and remnants grey,
Sweet-smelling, pale with poison, sanguine-hearted,
Passions that sprang from sleep and thoughts that started,
Shall death not bring us all as thee one day
Among the days departed?

VIII

For thee, O now a silent soul, my brother,
Take at my hands this garland, and farewell.
Thin is the leaf, and chill the wintry smell,
And chill the solemn earth, a fatal mother,
With sadder than the Niobean womb,
And in the hollow of her breasts a tomb.
Content thee, howsoe'er, whose days are done;
There lies not any troublous thing before,
Nor sight nor sound to war against thee more,
For whom all winds are quiet as the sun,
All waters as the shore.

Song

Love laid his sleepless head
On a thorny rosy bed;
And his eyes with tears were red,
And pale his lips as the dead.

And fear and sorrow and scorn
Kept watch by his head forlorn,
Till the night was overworn
And the world was merry with morn.

And Joy came up with the day
And kissed Love's lips as he lay,
And the watchers ghostly and grey
Sped from his pillow away.

And his eyes as the dawn grew bright,
And his lips waxed ruddy as light:
Sorrow may reign for a night,
But day shall bring back delight.

The Armada. 1588 : 1888

I

1

. . . For the light that abides upon England, the glory that rests on her godlike name,
The pride that is love and the love that is faith, a perfume dissolved in flame,
Took fire from the dawn of the fierce July when fleets were scattered as foam
And squadrons as flakes of spray; when galleon and galliass that shadowed the sea
Were swept from her waves like shadows that pass with the clouds they fell from, and she
Laughed loud to the wind as it gave to her keeping the glories of Spain and Rome.

II

Three hundred summers have fallen as leaves by the storms in their season thinned,
Since northward the war-ships of Spain came sheer up the way of the south-west wind:
Where the citadel cliffs of England are flanked with bastions of serpentine,
Far off to the windward loomed their hulls, an hundred and twenty-nine,
All filled full of the war, full-fraught with battle and charged with bale;
Then store-ships weighted with cannon; and all were an hundred and fifty sail.
The measureless menace of darkness anhungered with hope to prevail upon light,
The shadow of death made substance, the present and visible spirit of night,
Came, shaped as a waxing or waning moon that rose with the fall of day,
To the channel where couches the Lion in guard of the gate of the lustrous bay.
Fair England, sweet as the sea that shields her, and pure as the sea from stain,
Smiled, hearing hardly for scorn that stirred her the menace of saintly Spain.

II

...Full July in the fervent sky sets forth her twentieth of changing morns:
Winds fall mild that of late waxed wild: no presage whispers or wails or warns:
Far to west on the bland sea's breast a sailing crescent uprears her horns.

Seven wide miles the serene sea smiles between them stretching from rim to rim:
Soft they shine, but a darker sign should bid not hope or belief wax dim:
God's are these men, and not the sea's: their trust is set not on her but him.

God's? but who is the God whereto the prayers and incense of these men rise?
What is he, that the wind and sea should fear him, quelled by his sunbright eyes?
What, that men should return again, and hail him Lord of the servile skies?...

Ay, but we that the wind and sea gird round with shelter of storms and waves
Know not him that ye worship, grim as dreams that quicken from dead men's graves:
God is one with the sea, the sun, the land that nursed us, the love that saves.

Love whose heart is in ours, and part of all things noble and all things fair;
Sweet and free as the circling sea, sublime and kind as the fostering air;
Pure of shame as is England's name, whose crowns to come are as crowns that were.

III

...But the dusk of the day falls fruitless, whose light should have lit them on:
Sails flash through the gloom to shoreward, eclipsed as the sun that shone:
And the west wind wakes with dawn, and the hope that was here is gone.

Around they wheel and around, two knots to the Spaniard's one,
The wind-swift warriors of England, who shoot as with shafts of the sun,
With fourfold shots for the Spaniard's, that spare not till day be done.

And the wind with the sundown sharpens, and hurtles the ships to the lee,
And Spaniard on Spaniard smites, and shatters, and yields; and we,
Ere battle begin, stand lords of the battle, acclaimed of the sea.

And the day sweeps round to the nightward; and heavy and hard the waves
Roll in on the herd of the hurtling galleons; and masters and slaves
Reel blind in the grasp of the dark strong wind that shall dig their graves.

For the sepulchres hollowed and shaped of the wind in the swerve of the seas,
The graves that gape for their pasture, and laugh, thrilled through by the breeze,
The sweet soft merciless waters, await and are fain of these.

As the hiss of a Python heaving in menace of doom to be
They hear through the clear night round them, whose hours are as clouds that flee,
The whisper of tempest sleeping, the heave and the hiss of the sea.

But faith is theirs, and with faith are they girded and helmed and shod:
Invincible are they, almighty, elect for a sword and a rod;
Invincible even as their God is omnipotent, infinite, God.

In him is their strength, who have sworn that his glory shall wax not dim:
In his name are their war-ships hallowed as mightiest of all that swim:
The men that shall cope with these, and conquer, shall cast out him.

In him is the trust of their hearts; the desire of their eyes is he;
The light of their ways, made lightning for men that would fain be free:
Earth's hosts are with them, and with them is heaven: but with us is the sea.

IV

I

And a day and a night pass over;
  And the heart of their chief swells high;
For England, the warrior, the rover,
  Whose banners on all winds fly,
Soul-stricken, he saith, by the shadow of death, holds off him, and draws not nigh.

And the wind and the dawn together
  Make in from the gleaming east:
And fain of the wild glad weather
  As famine is fain of feast,
And fain of the fight, forth sweeps in its might the host of the Lord's high priest.

And lightly before the breeze
  The ships of his foes take wing:
Are they scattered, the lords of the seas?
  Are they broken, the foes of the king?
And ever now higher as a mounting fire the hopes of the Spaniard spring.

And a windless night comes down:
And a breezeless morning, bright
With promise of praise to crown
The close of the crowning fight,
Leaps up as the foe's heart leaps, and glows with lustrous rapture of light.

And stinted of gear for battle
The ships of the sea's folk lie,
Unwarlike, herded as cattle,
Six miles from the foeman's eye
That fastens as flame on the sight of them tame and offenceless, and ranged as to die.

Surely the souls in them quail,
They are stricken and withered at heart,
When in on them, sail by sail,
Fierce marvels of monstrous art,
Tower darkening on tower till the sea-winds cower crowds down as to hurl them apart.

And the windless weather is kindly,
And comforts the host in these;
And their hearts are uplift in them blindly,
And blindly they boast at ease
That the next day's fight shall exalt them, and smite with destruction the lords of the seas.

II

And lightly the proud hearts prattle,
And lightly the dawn draws nigh,
The dawn of the doom of the battle
When these shall falter and fly;
No day more great in the roll of fate filled ever with fire the sky.

To fightward they go as to feastward,
And the tempest of ships that drive
Sets eastward ever and eastward,
Till closer they strain and strive;
And the shots that rain on the hulls of Spain are as thunders afire and alive.

And about them the blithe sea smiles
And flashes to windward and lee
Round capes and headlands and isles
That heed not if war there be;
Round Sark, round Wight, green jewels of light in the ring of the golden sea.

But the men that within them abide
Are stout of spirit and stark
As rocks that repel the tide,
As days that repels the dark;
And the light bequeathed from their swords unsheathed shines lineal on Wight and on Sark.

And eastward the storm sets ever,
The storm of the sails that strain
And follow and close and sever
And lose and return and gain;
And English thunder divides in sunder the holds of the ships of Spain.

Southward to Calais, appalled
And astonished, the vast fleet veers;
And the skies are shrouded and palled,
But the moonless midnight hears
And sees how swift on them drive and drift strange flames that the darkness fears.

They fly through the night from shoreward,
Heart-stricken till morning break,
And ever to scourge them forward
Drives down on them England's Drake,
And hurls them in as they hurtle and spin and stagger, with storm to wake.

V

I

. . . Fierce noon beats hard on the battle; the galleons that loom to the lee
Bow down, heel over, uplifting their shelterless hulls from the sea:
From scuppers aspirt with blood, from guns dismounted and dumb,
The signs of the doom they looked for, the loud mute witnesses come.
They press with sunset to seaward for comfort: and shall not they find it there?
O servants of God most high, shall his winds not pass you by, and his waves not spare?

II

The wings of the south-west wind are widened; the breath of his fervent lips,
More keen than a sword's edge, fiercer than fire, falls full on the plunging ships.
The pilot is he of their northward flight, their stay and their steersman he;
A helmsman clothed with the tempest, and girdled with strength to constrain the sea.

And the host of them trembles and quails, caught fast in his
hand as a bird in the toils;
For the wrath and the joy that fulfil him are mightier than
man's, whom he slays and spoils.
And vainly, with heart divided in sunder, and labour of
wavering will,
The lord of their host takes counsel with hope if haply
their star shine still,
If haply some light be left them of chance to renew and
redeem the fray;
But the will of the black south-wester is lord of the councils
of war to-day.
One only spirit it quells not, a splendour undarkened of
chance or time;
Be the praise of his foes with Oquendo for ever, a name as
a star sublime.
But here what aid in a hero's heart, what help in his hand
may be?
For ever the dark wind whitens and blackens the hollows
and heights of the sea,
And galley by galley, divided and desolate, founders; and
none takes heed,
Nor foe nor friend, if they perish; forlorn, cast off in their
uttermost need,
They sink in the whelm of the waters, as pebbles by children from shoreward hurled,
In the North Sea's waters that end not, nor know they a
bourn but the bourn of the world.
Past many a secure unavailable harbour, and many a loud
stream's mouth,
Past Humber and Tees and Tyne and Tweed, they fly,
scourged on from the south;
For the wind, of its godlike mercy, relents not, and hounds
them ahead to the north,

With English hunters at heel, till now is the herd of them past the Forth,
All huddled and hurtled seaward; and now need none wage war upon these,
Nor huntsmen follow the quarry whose fall is the pastime sought of the seas.
Day upon day upon day confounds them, with measureless mists that swell,
With drift of rains everlasting and dense as the fumes of ascending hell.
Northward, and northward, and northward they stagger and shudder and swerve and flit,
Dismantled of masts and of yards, with sails by the fangs of the storm-wind split.
But north of the headland whose name is Wrath, by the wrath or the ruth of the sea,
They are swept or sustained to the westward, and drive through the rollers aloof to the lee.
Some strive yet northward for Iceland, and perish: but some through the storm-hewn straits
That sunder the Shetlands and Orkneys are borne of the breath which is God's or fate's:
And some, by the dawn of September, at last give thanks as for stars that smile,
For the winds have swept them to shelter and sight of the cliffs of a Catholic isle.
Though many the fierce rocks feed on, and many the merciless heretic slays,
Yet some that have laboured to land with their treasure are trustful, and give God praise.
And the kernes of murderous Ireland, athirst with a greed everlasting of blood,
Unslakable ever with slaughter and spoil, rage down as a ravening flood,

To slay and to flay of their shining apparel their brethren whom shipwreck spares;
Such faith and such mercy, such love and such manhood, such hands and such hearts are theirs.
And here, cast up from the ravening sea on the mild land's merciful breast,
This comfort they find of their fellows in worship; this guerdon is theirs of their quest.
Death was captain, and doom was pilot, and darkness the chart of their way;
Night and hell had in charge and in keeping the host of the foes of day.
Invincible, vanquished, impregnable, shattered, a sign to her foes of fear,
A sign to the world and the stars of laughter, the fleet of the Lord lies here.
Nay, for none may declare the place of the ruin wherein she lies;
Nay, for none hath beholden the grave whence never a ghost shall rise.
The fleet of the foemen of England hath found not one but a thousand graves;
And he that shall number and name them shall number by name and by tale the waves.

VI

...England, queen of the waves whose green inviolate girdle enrings thee round,
Mother fair as the morning, where is now the place of thy foemen found?
Still the sea that salutes us free proclaims them stricken, acclaims thee crowned.

Times may change, and the skies grow strange with signs
of treason and fraud and fear:
Foes in union of strange communion may rise against thee
from far and near:
Sloth and greed on thy strength may feed as cankers waxing
from year to year.

Yet, though treason and fierce unreason should league and
lie and defame and smite,
We that know thee, how far below thee the hatred burns of
the sons of night,
We that love thee, behold above thee the witness written
of life in light.

Life that shines from thee shows forth signs that none may
read not but eyeless foes:
Hate, born blind, in his abject mind grows hopeful now
but as madness grows:
Love, born wise, with exultant eyes adores thy glory,
beholds and glows.

Truth is in thee, and none may win thee to lie, forsaking
the face of truth:
Freedom lives by the grace she gives thee, born again from
thy deathless youth:
Faith should fail, and the world turn pale, wert thou the
prey of the serpent's tooth.

Greed and fraud, unabashed, unawed, may strive to sting
thee at heel in vain:
Craft and fear and mistrust may leer and mourn and murmur and plead and plain:
Thou art thou: and thy sunbright brow is hers that blasted
the strength of Spain.

Mother, mother beloved, none other could claim in place of thee England's place:
Earth bears none that beholds the sun so pure of record, so clothed with grace:
Dear our mother, nor son nor brother is thine, as strong or as fair of face.

How shalt thou be abased? or how shall fear take hold of thy heart? of thine,
England, maiden immortal, laden with charge of life and with hopes divine?
Earth shall wither, when eyes turned hither behold not light in her darkness shine.

England, none that is born thy son, and lives, by grace of thy glory, free,
Lives and yearns not at heart and burns with hope to serve as he worships thee;
None may sing thee: the sea-wind's wing beats down our songs as it hails the sea.

To a Seamew

When I had wings, my brother,
  Such wings were mine as thine:
Such life my heart remembers
In all as wild Septembers
As this when life seems other,
  Though sweet, than once was mine;
When I had wings, my brother,
  Such wings were mine as thine.

Such life as thrills and quickens
  The silence of thy flight,
Or fills thy note's elation
With lordlier exultation

Than man's, whose faint heart sickens
   With hopes and fears that blight
Such life as thrills and quickens
   The silence of thy flight.

Thy cry from windward clanging
   Makes all the cliffs rejoice;
Though storm clothe seas with sorrow,
Thy call salutes the morrow;
While shades of pain seem hanging
   Round earth's most rapturous voice,
Thy cry from windward clanging
   Makes all the cliffs rejoice.

We, sons and sires of seamen,
   Whose home is all the sea,
What place man may, we claim it;
But thine—whose thought may name it?
Free birds live higher than freemen,
   And gladlier ye than we—
We, sons and sires of seamen,
   Whose home is all the sea.

For you the storm sounds only
   More notes of more delight
Than earth's in sunniest weather:
When heaven and sea together
Join strengths against the lonely
   Lost bark borne down by night,
For you the storm sounds only
   More notes of more delight.

With wider wing, and louder
   Long clarion-call of joy,
Thy tribe salutes the terror
Of darkness, wild as error,

But sure as truth, and prouder
  Than waves with man for toy;
With wider wing, and louder
  Long clarion-call of joy.

The wave's wing spreads and flutters,
  The wave's heart swells and breaks;
One moment's passion thrills it,
One pulse of power fulfils it
And ends the pride it utters
  When, loud with life that quakes,
The wave's wing spreads and flutters,
  The wave's heart swells and breaks.

But thine and thou, my brother,
  Keep heart and wing more high
Than aught may scare or sunder;
The waves whose throats are thunder
Fall hurtling each on other,
  And triumph as they die;
But thine and thou, my brother,
  Keep heart and wing more high.

More high than wrath or anguish,
  More strong than pride or fear,
The sense or soul half hidden
In thee, for us forbidden,
Bids thee nor change nor languish,
  But live thy life as here,
More high than wrath or anguish,
  More strong than pride or fear.

We are fallen, even we, whose passion
  On earth is nearest thine;
Who sing, and cease from flying;
Who live, and dream of dying:

Grey time, in time's grey fashion,
  Bids wingless creatures pine:
We are fallen, even we, whose passion
  On earth is nearest thine.

The lark knows no such rapture,
  Such joy no nightingale,
As sways the songless measure
Wherein thy wings take pleasure:
Thy love may no man capture,
  Thy pride may no man quail;
The lark knows no such rapture,
  Such joy no nightingale.

And we, whom dreams embolden,
  We can but creep and sing
And watch through heaven's waste hollow
The flight no sight may follow
To the utter bourne beholden
  Of none that lack thy wing:
And we, whom dreams embolden,
  We can but creep and sing.

Our dreams have wings that falter,
  Our hearts bear hopes that die;
For thee no dream could better
A life no fears may fetter,
A pride no care can alter,
  That wots not whence or why
Our dreams have wings that falter,
  Our hearts bear hopes that die.

With joy more fierce and sweeter
  Than joys we deem divine
Their lives, by time untarnished,
Are girt about and garnished,

Who match the wave's full metre
And drink the wind's wild wine
With joy more fierce and sweeter
Than joys we deem divine.

Ah, well were I for ever,
Wouldst thou change lives with me,
And take my song's wild honey,
And give me back thy sunny
Wide eyes that weary never,
And wings that search the sea;
Ah, well were I for ever,
Wouldst thou change lives with me.

In a Garden

Baby, see the flowers!
—Baby sees
Fairer things than these,
Fairer though they be than dreams of ours.

Baby, hear the birds!
—Baby knows
Better songs than those,
Sweeter though they sound than sweetest words.

Baby, see the moon!
—Baby's eyes
Laugh to watch it rise,
Answering light with love and night with noon.

Baby, hear the sea!
—Baby's face
Takes a graver grace,
Touched with wonder what the sound may be.

Baby, see the star!
—Baby's hand
Opens, warm and bland,
Calm in claim of all things fair that are.

Baby, hear the bells!
—Baby's head
Bows, as ripe for bed,
Now the flowers curl round and close their cells.

Baby, flower of light,
Sleep, and see
Brighter dreams than we,
Till good day shall smile away good night.

The Winds

O weary fa' the east wind,
And weary fa' the west:
And gin I were under the wan waves wide
I wot weel wad I rest.

O weary fa' the north wind,
And weary fa' the south:
The sea went ower my good lord's head
Or ever he kissed my mouth.

Weary fa' the windward rocks,
And weary fa' the lee:
They might hae sunken sevenscore ships,
And let my love's gang free.

And weary fa' ye, mariners a',
And weary fa' the sea:
It might hae taken an hundred men,
And let my ae love be.

The Bride's Tragedy

"The wind wears roun', the day wears doun,
  The moon is grisly grey;
There's nae man rides by the mirk muirsides,
  Nor down the dark Tyne's way."
    In, in, out and in,
    Blaws the wind and whirls the whin.

"And winna ye watch the night wi' me,
  And winna ye wake the morn?
Foul shame it were that your ae mither
  Should brook her ae son's scorn."

"O mither, I may not sleep nor stay,
  My weird is ill to dree;
For a fause faint lord of the south seaboard
  Wad win my bride of me."

"The winds are strang, and the nights are lang,
  And the ways are sair to ride:
And I maun gang to wreak my wrang,
  And ye maun bide and bide."

"Gin I maun bide and bide, Willie,
  I wot my weird is sair:
Weel may ye get ye a light love yet,
  But never a mither mair."

"O gin the morrow be great wi' sorrow,
  The wyte be yours of a':
But though ye slay me that haud and stay me,
  The weird ye will maun fa'."

When cocks were crawing and day was dawing,
  He's boun' him forth to ride:
And the ae first may he's met that day
  Was fause Earl Robert's bride.

O blithe and braw were the bride-folk a',
  But sad and saft rade she;
And sad as doom was her fause bridegroom,
  But fair and fain was he.

"And winna ye bide, sae saft ye ride,
  And winna ye speak wi' me?
For mony's the word and the kindly word
  I have spoken aft wi' thee."

"My lamp was lit yestreen, Willie,
  My window-gate was wide:
But ye camena nigh me till day came by me
  And made me not your bride."

He's set his hand to her bridle-rein,
  He's turned her horse away:
And the cry was sair, and the wrath was mair,
  And fast and fain rode they.

But when they came by Chollerford,
  I wot the ways were fell;
For broad and brown the spate swang down,
  And the lift was mirk as hell.

"And will ye ride yon fell water,
  Or will ye bide for fear?
Nae scathe ye'll win o' your father's kin,
  Though they should slay me here."

"I had liefer ride yon fell water,
  Though strange it be to ride,
Than I wad stand on the fair green strand
  And thou be slain beside."

"I had liefer swim yon wild water,
  Though sair it be to bide,
Than I wad stand at a strange man's hand,
  To be a strange man's bride."

"I had liefer drink yon dark water,
  Wi' the stanes to make my bed,
And the faem to hide me, and thou beside me,
  Than I wad see thee dead."

He's kissed her twice, he's kissed her thrice,
  On cheek and lip and chin:
He's wound her rein to his hand again,
  And lightly they leapt in.

Their hearts were high to live or die,
  Their steeds were stark of limb:
But the stream was starker, the spate was darker,
  Than man might live and swim.

The first ae step they strode therein,
  It smote them foot and knee:
But ere they wan to the mid water
  The spate was as the sea.

But when they wan to the mid water,
  It smote them hand and head:
And nae man knows but the wave that flows
  Where they lie drowned and dead.
    In, in, out and in,
    Blaws the wind and whirls the whin.

A Jacobite's Exile

1746

The weary day rins down and dies,
  The weary night wears through:
And never an hour is fair wi' flower,
  And never a flower wi' dew.

I would the day were night for me,
  I would the night were day:
For then would I stand in my ain fair land,
  As now in dreams I may.

O lordly flow the Loire and Seine,
  And loud the dark Durance:
But bonnier shine the braes of Tyne
  Than a' the fields of France;
And the waves of Till that speak sae still
  Gleam goodlier where they glance.

O weel were they that fell fighting
  On dark Drumossie's day:
They keep their hame ayont the faem,
  And we die far away.

O sound they sleep, and saft, and deep,
  But night and day wake we;
And ever between the sea-banks green
  Sounds loud the sundering sea.

And ill we sleep, sae sair we weep,
  But sweet and fast sleep they;
And the mool that haps them roun' and laps them
  Is e'en their country's clay;
But the land we tread that are not dead
  Is strange as night by day.

Strange as night in a strange man's sight,
  Though fair as dawn it be:
For what is here that a stranger's cheer
  Should yet wax blithe to see?

The hills stand steep, the dells lie deep,
  The fields are green and gold:
The hill-streams sing, and the hill-sides ring,
  As ours at home of old.

But hills and flowers are nane of ours,
  And ours are oversea:
And the kind strange land whereon we stand,
  It wotsna what were we
Or ever we came, wi' scathe and shame,
  To try what end might be.

Scathe, and shame, and a waefu' name,
  And a weary time and strange,
Have they that seeing a weird for dreeing
  Can die, and cannot change.

Shame and scorn may we thole that mourn,
  Though sair be they to dree:
But ill may we bide the thoughts we hide,
  Mair keen than wind and sea.

Ill may we thole the night's watches,
  And ill the weary day:
And the dreams that keep the gates of sleep,
  A waefu' gift gie they;
For the sangs they sing us, the sights they bring us,
  The morn blaws all away.

On Aikenshaw the sun blinks braw,
  The burn rins blithe and fain:
There's nought wi' me I wadna gie
  To look thereon again.

On Keilder-side the wind blaws wide;
  There sounds nae hunting-horn
That rings sae sweet as the winds that beat
  Round banks where Tyne is born.

The Wansbeck sings with all her springs,
  The bents and braes give ear;

But the wood that rings wi' the sang she sings
I may not see nor hear;
For far and far thae blithe burns are,
And strange is a' thing near.

The light there lightens, the day there brightens,
The loud wind there lives free:
Nae light comes nigh me or wind blaws by me
That I wad hear or see.

But O gin I were there again,
Afar ayont the faem,
Cauld and dead in the sweet saft bed
That haps my sires at hame!

We'll see nae mair the sea-banks fair,
And the sweet grey gleaming sky,
And the lordly strand of Northumberland,
And the goodly towers thereby:
And none shall know but the winds that blow
The graves wherein we lie.

Thalassius

..."Child of my sunlight and the sea, from birth
A fosterling and fugitive on earth;
Sleepless of soul as wind or wave or fire,
A manchild with an ungrown God's desire;
Because thou hast loved nought mortal more than me,
Thy father, and thy mother-hearted sea;
Because thou hast set thine heart to sing, and sold
Life and life's love for song, God's living gold;
Because thou hast given thy flower and fire of youth
To feed men's hearts with visions, truer than truth;

Because thou hast kept in those world-wandering eyes
The light that makes me music of the skies;
Because thou hast heard with world-unwearied ears
The music that puts light into the spheres;
Have therefore in thine heart and in thy mouth
The sound of song that mingles north and south,
The song of all the winds that sing of me,
And in thy soul the sense of all the sea."

Prelude

Between the green bud and the red
Youth sat and sang by Time, and shed
  From eyes and tresses flowers and tears,
  From heart and spirit hopes and fears,
Upon the hollow stream whose bed
  Is channelled by the foamless years;
And with the white the gold-haired head
  Mixed running locks, and in Time's ears
Youth's dreams hung singing, and Time's truth
Was half not harsh in the ears of Youth.

Between the bud and the blown flower
Youth talked with joy and grief an hour,
  With footless joy and wingless grief
  And twin-born faith and disbelief
Who share the seasons to devour;
  And long ere these made up their sheaf
Felt the winds round him shake and shower
  The rose-red and the blood-red leaf,
Delight whose germ grew never grain,
And passion dyed in its own pain.

Then he stood up, and trod to dust
Fear and desire, mistrust and trust,
And dreams of bitter sleep and sweet,
And bound for sandals on his feet
Knowledge and patience of what must
And what things may be, in the heat
And cold of years that rot and rust
And alter; and his spirit's meat
Was freedom, and his staff was wrought
Of strength, and his cloak woven of thought.

For what has he whose will sees clear
To do with doubt and faith and fear,
Swift hopes and slow despondencies?
His heart is equal with the sea's
And with the sea-wind's, and his ear
Is level to the speech of these,
And his soul communes and takes cheer
With the actual earth's equalities,
Air, light, and night, hills, winds, and streams,
And seeks not strength from strengthless dreams.

His soul is even with the sun
Whose spirit and whose eye are one,
Who seeks not stars by day, nor light
And heavy heat of day by night.
Him can no God cast down, whom none
Can lift in hope beyond the height
Of fate and nature and things done
By the calm rule of might and right
That bids men be and bear and do,
And die beneath blind skies or blue.

To him the lights of even and morn
Speak no vain things of love or scorn,

Fancies and passions miscreate
By man in things dispassionate.
Nor holds he fellowship forlorn
With souls that pray and hope and hate,
And doubt they had better not been born,
And fain would lure or scare off fate
And charm their doomsman from their doom
And make fear dig its own false tomb.

He builds not half of doubts and half
Of dreams his own soul's cenotaph,
Whence hopes and fears with helpless eyes,
Wrapt loose in cast-off cerecloths, rise
And dance and wring their hands and laugh,
And weep thin tears and sigh light sighs,
And without living lips would quaff
The living spring in man that lies,
And drain his soul of faith and strength
It might have lived on a life's length.

He hath given himself and hath not sold
To God for heaven or man for gold,
Or grief for comfort that it gives,
Or joy for grief's restoratives.
He hath given himself to time, whose fold
Shuts in the mortal flock that lives
On its plain pasture's heat and cold
And the equal year's alternatives.
Earth, heaven, and time, death, life, and he,
Endure while they shall be to be.

"Yet between death and life are hours
To flush with love and hide in flowers;
What profit save in these?" men cry:
"Ah see, between soft earth and sky,

What only good things here are ours!"
  They say, "what better wouldst thou try,
What sweeter sing of? or what powers
  Serve, that will give thee ere thou die
More joy to sing and be less sad,
More heart to play and grow more glad?"

Play then and sing; we too have played,
We likewise, in that subtle shade.
  We too have twisted through our hair
  Such tendrils as the wild Loves wear,
And heard what mirth the Mænads made,
  Till the wind blew our garlands bare
And left their roses disarrayed,
  And smote the summer with strange air,
And disengirdled and discrowned
The limbs and locks that vine-wreaths bound.

* * * * * *

For Pleasure slumberless and pale,
And Passion with rejected veil,
  Pass, and the tempest-footed throng
  Of hours that follow them with song
Till their feet flag and voices fail,
  And lips that were so loud so long
Learn silence, or a wearier wail;
  So keen is change, and time so strong,
To weave the robes of life and rend
And weave again till life have end.

But weak is change, but strengthless time,
To take the light from heaven, or climb
  The hills of heaven with wasting feet.
  Songs they can stop that earth found meet,

But the stars keep their ageless rhyme;
  Flowers they can slay that spring thought sweet,
But the stars keep their spring sublime;
  Passions and pleasures can defeat,
Actions and agonies control,
And life and death, but not the soul.

Because man's soul is man's God still,
What wind soever waft his will
  Across the waves of day and night
  To port or shipwreck, left or right,
By shores and shoals of good and ill;
  And still its flame at mainmast height
Through the rent air that foam-flakes fill
  Sustains the indomitable light
Whence only man hath strength to steer
Or helm to handle without fear.

Save his own soul's light overhead,
None leads him, and none ever led,
  Across birth's hidden harbour-bar,
  Past youth where shoreward shallows are,
Through age that drives on toward the red
  Vast void of sunset hailed from far,
To the equal waters of the dead;
  Save his own soul he hath no star,
And sinks, except his own soul guide,
Helmless in middle turn of tide.

No blast of air or fire of sun
Puts out the light whereby we run
  With girded loins our lamplit race,
  And each from each takes heart of grace

And spirit till his turn be done,
  And light of face from each man's face
In whom the light of trust is one;
  Since only souls that keep their place
By their own light, and watch things roll,
And stand, have light for any soul.

A little time we gain from time
To set our seasons in some chime,
  For harsh or sweet or loud or low,
  With seasons played out long ago
And souls that in their time and prime
  Took part with summer or with snow,
Lived abject lives out or sublime,
  And had their chance of seed to sow
For service or disservice done
To those days dead and this their son.

A little time that we may fill
Or with such good works or such ill
  As loose the bonds or make them strong
  Wherein all manhood suffers wrong.
By rose-hung river and light-foot rill
  There are who rest not; who think long
Till they discern as from a hill
  At the sun's hour of morning song,
Known of souls only, and those souls free.
The sacred spaces of the sea.

A Watch in the Night

Watchman, what of the night?—
  Storm and thunder and rain,
  Lights that waver and wane,
Leaving the watchfires unlit.

Only the balefires are bright,
And the flash of the lamps now and then
From a palace where spoilers sit,
Trampling the children of men.

Prophet, what of the night?—
I stand by the verge of the sea,
Banished, uncomforted, free,
Hearing the noise of the waves
And sudden flashes that smite
Some man's tyrannous head,
Thundering, heard among graves
That hide the hosts of his dead.

Mourners, what of the night?—
All night through without sleep
We weep, and we weep, and we weep.
Who shall give us our sons?
Beaks of raven and kite,
Mouths of wolf and of hound,
Give us them back whom the guns
Shot for you dead on the ground.

Dead men, what of the night?—
Cannon and scaffold and sword,
Horror of gibbet and cord,
Mowed us as sheaves for the grave,
Mowed us down for the right.
We do not grudge or repent.
Freely to freedom we gave
Pledges, till life should be spent.

Statesman, what of the night?—
The night will last me my time.
The gold on a crown or a crime
Looks well enough yet by the lamps.

Have we not fingers to write,
  Lips to swear at a need?
Then, when danger decamps,
  Bury the word with the deed.

Warrior, what of the night?—
  Whether it be not or be
  Night, is as one thing to me.
I for one, at the least,
Ask not of dews if they blight,
  Ask not of flames if they slay,
Ask not of prince or of priest
  How long ere we put them away.

Master, what of the night?—
  Child, night is not at all
  Anywhere, fallen or to fall,
Save in our star-stricken eyes.
Forth of our eyes it takes flight,
  Look we but once nor before
Nor behind us, but straight on the skies;
  Night is not then any more.

Exile, what of the night?—
  The tides and the hours run out,
  The seasons of death and of doubt,
The night-watches bitter and sore.
In the quicksands leftward and right
  My feet sink down under me;
But I know the scents of the shore
  And the broad blown breaths of the sea.

Captives, what of the night?—
  It rains outside overhead
  Always, a rain that is red,
And our faces are soiled with the rain.

Here in the seasons' despite
   Day-time and night-time are one,
Till the curse of the kings and the chain
   Break, and their toils be undone.

Christian, what of the night?—
   I cannot tell; I am blind.
   I halt and hearken behind
If haply the hours will go back
And return to the dear dead light,
   To the watchfires and stars that of old
Shone where the sky now is black,
   Glowed where the earth now is cold.

High priest, what of the night?—
   The night is horrible here
   With haggard faces and fear,
Blood, and the burning of fire.
Mine eyes are emptied of sight,
   Mine hands are full of the dust.
If the God of my faith be a liar,
   Who is it that I shall trust?

Princes, what of the night?—
   Night with pestilent breath
   Feeds us, children of death,
Clothes us close with her gloom.
Rapine and famine and fright
   Crouch at our feet and are fed.
Earth where we pass is a tomb,
   Life where we triumph is dead.

Martyrs, what of the night?—
   Nay, is it night with you yet?
   We, for our part, we forget
What night was, if it were.

The loud red mouths of the fight
  Are silent and shut where we are.
In our eyes the tempestuous air
  Shines as the face of a star.

England, what of the night?—
  Night is for slumber and sleep,
  Warm, no season to weep.
Let me alone till the day.
Sleep would I still if I might,
  Who have slept for two hundred years.
Once I had honour, they say;
  But slumber is sweeter than tears....

Liberty, what of the night?—
  I feel not the red rains fall,
  Hear not the tempest at all,
Nor thunder in heaven any more.
All the distance is white
  With the soundless feet of the sun.
Night, with the woes that it wore,
  Night is over and done.

To Walt Whitman in America

Send but a song oversea for us,
  Heart of their hearts who are free,
Heart of their singer, to be for us
  More than our singing can be;
Ours, in the tempest at error,
With no light but the twilight of terror;
  Send us a song oversea!

Sweet-smelling of pine-leaves and grasses,
  And blown as a tree through and through
With the winds of the keen mountain-passes,
  And tender as sun-smitten dew;
Sharp-tongued as the winter that shakes
The wastes of your limitless lakes,
  Wide-eyed as the sea-line's blue.

O strong-winged soul with prophetic
  Lips hot with the bloodbeats of song,
With tremor of heartstrings magnetic,
  With thoughts as thunders in throng,
With consonant ardours of chords
That pierce men's souls as with swords
  And hale them hearing along,

Make us too music, to be with us
  As a word from a world's heart warm,
To sail the dark as a sea with us,
  Full-sailed, outsinging the storm,
A song to put fire in our ears
Whose burning shall burn up tears,
  Whose sign bid battle reform;

A note in the ranks of a clarion,
  A word in the wind of cheer,
To consume as with lightning the carrion
  That makes time foul for us here;
In the air that our dead things infest
A blast of the breath of the west,
  Till east way as west way is clear.

Out of the sun beyond sunset,
  From the evening whence morning shall be,
With the rollers in measureless onset,
  With the van of the storming sea,

With the world-wide wind, with the breath
That breaks ships driven upon death,
  With the passion of all things free,

With the sea-steeds footless and frantic,
  White myriads for death to bestride
In the charge of the ruining Atlantic
  Where deaths by regiments ride,
With clouds and clamours of waters,
With a long note shriller than slaughter's
  On the furrowless fields world-wide,

With terror, with ardour and wonder,
  With the soul of the season that wakes
When the weight of a whole year's thunder
  In the tidestream of autumn breaks,
Let the flight of the wide-winged word
Come over, come in and be heard,
  Take form and fire for our sakes.

For a continent bloodless with travail
  Here toils and brawls as it can,
And the web of it who shall unravel
  Of all that peer on the plan;
Would fain grow men, but they grow not,
And fain be free, but they know not
  One name for freedom and man?

One name, not twain for division;
  One thing, not twain, from the birth;
Spirit and substance and vision,
  Worth more than worship is worth;
Unbeheld, unadored, undivined,
The cause, the centre, the mind,
  The secret and sense of the earth.

Here as a weakling in irons,
  Here as a weanling in bands,
As a prey that the stake-net environs,
  Our life that we looked for stands;
And the man-child naked and dear,
Democracy, turns on us here
  Eyes trembling with tremulous hands.

* * * * * *

Round your people and over them
  Light like raiment is drawn,
Close as a garment to cover them
  Wrought not of mail nor of lawn;
Here, with hope hardly to wear,
Naked nations and bare
  Swim, sink, strike out for the dawn.

Chains are here, and a prison,
  Kings, and subjects, and shame;
If the God upon you be arisen,
  How should our songs be the same?
How, in confusion of change,
How shall we sing, in a strange
  Land, songs praising his name?

God is buried and dead to us,
  Even the spirit of earth,
Freedom; so have they said to us,
  Some with mocking and mirth,
Some with heartbreak and tears;
And a God without eyes, without ears,
  Who shall sing of him, dead in the birth?

* * * * * *

But in weariest of years and obscurest
  Doth it live not at heart of all things,

The one God and one spirit, a purest
  Life, fed from unstanchable springs?
Within love, within hatred it is,
And its seed in the stripe as the kiss,
  And in slaves is the germ, and in kings.

Freedom we call it, for holier
  Name of the soul's there is none;
Surelier it labours, if slowlier,
  Than the metres of star or of sun;
Slowlier than life into breath,
Surelier than time into death,
  It moves till its labour be done.

Till the motion be done and the measure
  Circling through season and clime,
Slumber and sorrow and pleasure,
  Vision of virtue and crime;
Till consummate with conquering eyes,
A soul disembodied, it rise
  From the body transfigured of time.

Till it rise and remain and take station
  With the stars of the worlds that rejoice;
Till the voice of its heart's exultation
  Be as theirs an invariable voice;
By no discord of evil estranged,
By no pause, by no breach in it changed,
  By no clash in the chord of its choice.

It is one with the world's generations,
  With the spirit, the star, and the sod;
With the kingless and king-stricken nations,
  With the cross, and the chain, and the rod;
The most high, the most secret, most lonely,
The earth-soul Freedom, that only
  Lives, and that only is God.

Mater Triumphalis

Mother of man's time-travelling generations,
Breath of his nostrils, heartblood of his heart,
God above all Gods worshipped of all nations,
Light above light, law beyond law, thou art.

Thy face is as a sword smiting in sunder
Shadows and chains and dreams and iron things;
The sea is dumb before thy face, the thunder
Silent, the skies are narrower than thy wings.

Angels and Gods, spirit and sense, thou takest
In thy right hand as drops of dust or dew;
The temples and the towers of time thou breakest,
His thoughts and words and works, to make them new.

All we have wandered from thy ways, have hidden
Eyes from thy glory and ears from calls they heard;
Called of thy trumpets vainly, called and chidden,
Scourged of thy speech and wounded of thy word.

We have known thee and have not known thee; stood beside thee,
Felt thy lips breathe, set foot where thy feet trod,
Loved and renounced and worshipped and denied thee,
As though thou wert but as another God.

"One hour for sleep," we said, "and yet one other;
All day we served her, and who shall serve by night?"
Not knowing of thee, thy face not knowing, O mother,
O light wherethrough the darkness is as light.

Men that forsook thee hast thou not forsaken,
Races of men that knew not hast thou known;
Nations that slept thou hast doubted not to waken,
Worshippers of strange Gods to make thine own.

All old grey histories hiding thy clear features,
O secret spirit and sovereign, all men's tales,
Creeds woven of men thy children and thy creatures,
They have woven for vestures of thee and for veils.

Thine hands, without election or exemption,
Feed all men fainting from false peace or strife,
O thou, the resurrection and redemption,
The godhead and the manhood and the life.

Thy wings shadow the waters; thine eyes lighten
The horror of the hollows of the night;
The depths of the earth and the dark places brighten
Under thy feet, whiter than fire is white.

Death is subdued to thee, and hell's bands broken;
Where thou art only is heaven; who hears not thee,
Time shall not hear him; when men's names are spoken,
A nameless sign of death shall his name be.

Deathless shall be the death, the name be nameless;
Sterile of stars his twilight time of breath;
With fire of hell shall shame consume him shameless,
And dying, all the night darken his death.

The years are as thy garments, the world's ages
As sandals bound and loosed from thy swift feet;
Time serves before thee, as one that hath for wages
Praise or shame only, bitter words or sweet.

* * * * * *

Through the iron years, the centuries brazen-gated,
By the ages' barred impenetrable doors,
From the evening to the morning have we waited,
Should thy foot haply sound on the awful floors.

The floors untrodden of the sun's feet glimmer,
  The star-unstricken pavements of the night;
Do the lights burn inside? the lights wax dimmer
  On festal faces withering out of sight.

The crowned heads lose the light on them; it may be
  Dawn is at hand to smite the loud feast dumb;
To blind the torch-lit centuries till the day be,
  The feasting kingdoms till thy kingdom come.

Shall it not come? deny they or dissemble,
  Is it not even as lightning from on high
Now? and though many a soul close eyes and tremble,
  How should they tremble at all who love thee as I?

I am thine harp between thine hands, O mother!
  All my strong chords are strained with love of thee.
We grapple in love and wrestle, as each with other
  Wrestle the wind and the unreluctant sea.

I am no courtier of thee sober-suited,
  Who loves a little for a little pay.
Me not thy winds and storms nor thrones disrooted
  Nor molten crowns nor thine own sins dismay.

* * * * * *

I do not bid thee spare me, O dreadful mother!
  I pray thee that thou spare not, of thy grace.
How were it with me then, if ever another
  Should come to stand before thee in this my place?

I am the trumpet at thy lips, thy clarion
  Full of thy cry, sonorous with thy breath;
The graves of souls born worms and creeds grown carrion
  Thy blast of judgment fills with fires of death.

Thou art the player whose organ-keys are thunders,
And I beneath thy foot the pedal prest;
Thou art the ray whereat the rent night sunders,
And I the cloudlet borne upon thy breast.

I shall burn up before thee, pass and perish,
As haze in sunrise on the red sea-line;
But thou from dawn to sunsetting shalt cherish
The thoughts that led and souls that lighted mine.

* * * * * *

I have no spirit of skill with equal fingers
At sign to sharpen or to slacken strings;
I keep no time of song with gold-perched singers
And chirp of linnets on the wrists of kings.

I am thy storm-thrush of the days that darken,
Thy petrel in the foam that bears thy bark
To port through night and tempest; if thou hearken,
My voice is in thy heaven before the lark.

My song is in the mist that hides thy morning,
My cry is up before the day for thee;
I have heard thee and beheld thee and give warning,
Before thy wheels divide the sky and sea.

* * * * * *

Come, though all heaven again be fire above thee;
Though death before thee come to clear thy sky;
Let us but see in his thy face who love thee;
Yea, though thou slay us, arise and let us die.

Cor Cordium

O heart of hearts, the chalice of love's fire,
Hid round with flowers and all the bounty of bloom;
O wonderful and perfect heart, for whom
The lyrist liberty made life a lyre;
O heavenly heart, at whose most dear desire
Dead love, living and singing, cleft his tomb,
And with him risen and regent in death's room
All day thy choral pulses rang full choir;
O heart whose beating blood was running song,
O sole thing sweeter than thine own songs were,
Help us for thy free love's sake to be free,
True for thy truth's sake, for thy strength's sake strong,
Till very liberty make clean and fair
The nursing earth as the sepulchral sea.

Perinde ac Cadaver

In a vision Liberty stood
By the childless charm-stricken bed
Where, barren of glory and good,
Knowing nought if she would not or would,
England slept with her dead.

Her face that the foam had whitened,
Her hands that were strong to strive,
Her eyes whence battle had lightened,
Over all was a drawn shroud tightened
To bind her asleep and alive.

She turned and laughed in her dream
With grey lips arid and cold;
She saw not the face as a beam
Burn on her, but only a gleam
Through her sleep as of new-stamped gold.

But the goddess, with terrible tears
In the light of her down-drawn eyes,
Spake fire in the dull sealed ears;
"Thou, sick with slumbers and fears,
Wilt thou sleep now indeed or arise?

"With dreams and with words and with light
Memories and empty desires
Thou hast wrapped thyself round all night;
Thou hast shut up thine heart from the right,
And warmed thee at burnt-out fires.

"Yet once if I smote at thy gate,
Thy sons would sleep not, but heard;
O thou that wast found so great,
Art thou smitten with folly or fate
That thy sons have forgotten my word?

"O Cromwell's mother, O breast
That suckled Milton! thy name
That was beautiful then, that was blest,
Is it wholly discrowned and deprest,
Trodden under by sloth into shame?

"Why wilt thou hate me and die?
For none can hate me and live.
What ill have I done to thee? why
Wilt thou turn from me fighting, and fly,
Who would follow thy feet and forgive?

"Thou hast seen me stricken, and said,
What is it to me? I am strong:
Thou hast seen me bowed down on my dead
And laughed and lifted thine head,
And washed thine hands of my wrong.

"Thou hast put out the soul of thy sight;
  Thou hast sought to my foemen as friend,
To my traitors that kiss me and smite,
To the kingdoms and empires of night
  That begin with the darkness, and end.

"Turn thee, awaken, arise,
  With the light that is risen on the lands,
With the change of the fresh-coloured skies;
Set thine eyes on mine eyes,
  Lay thy hands in my hands."

She moved and mourned as she heard,
  Sighed and shifted her place,
As the wells of her slumber were stirred
By the music and wind of the word,
  Then turned and covered her face.

"Ah," she said in her sleep,
  "Is my work not done with and done?
Is there corn for my sickle to reap?
And strange is the pathway, and steep,
  And sharp overhead is the sun.

"I have done thee service enough,
  Loved thee enough in my day;
Now nor hatred nor love
Nor hardly remembrance thereof
  Lives in me to lighten my way.

"And is it not well with us here?
  Is change as good as is rest?
What hope should move me, or fear,
That eye should open or ear,
  Who have long since won what is best?

"Where among us are such things
As turn men's hearts into hell?
Have we not queens without stings,
Scotched princes, and fangless kings?
Yea," she said, "we are well.

"We have filed the teeth of the snake
Monarchy, how should it bite?
Should the slippery slow thing wake,
It will not sting for my sake;
Yea," she said, "I do right."

So spake she, drunken with dreams,
Mad; but again in her ears
A voice as of storm-swelled streams
Spake; "No brave shame then redeems
Thy lusts of sloth and thy fears?

"Thy poor lie slain of thine hands,
Their starved limbs rot in thy sight;
As a shadow the ghost of thee stands
Among men living and lands,
And stirs not leftward or right.

"Freeman he is not, but slave,
Who stands not out on my side;
His own hand hollows his grave,
Nor strength is in me to save
Where strength is none to abide.

"Time shall tread on his name
That was written for honour of old,
Who hath taken in change for fame
Dust, and silver, and shame,
Ashes, and iron, and gold."

The Oblation

Ask nothing more of me, sweet;
 All I can give you I give.
  Heart of my heart, were it more,
More would be laid at your feet:
 Love that should help you to live,
  Song that should spur you to soar.

All things were nothing to give
 Once to have sense of you more,
  Touch you and taste of you sweet,
Think you and breathe you and live,
 Swept of your wings as they soar,
  Trodden by chance of your feet.

I that have love and no more
 Give you but love of you, sweet:
  He that hath more, let him give;
He that hath wings, let him soar;
 Mine is the heart at your feet
  Here, that must love you to live.

Tristram of Lyonesse

STORM IN "THE SAILING OF THE SWALLOW"

And while they sat at speech as at a feast,
Came a light wind fast hardening forth of the east
And blackening till its might had marred the skies;
And the sea thrilled as with heart-sundering sighs
One after one drawn, with each breath it drew,
And the green hardened into iron blue,
And the soft light went out of all its face.
Then Tristram girt him for an oarsman's place

And took his oar and smote, and toiled with might
In the east wind's full face and the strong sea's spite
Labouring; and all the rowers rowed hard, but he
More mightily than any wearier three.
And Iseult watched him rowing with sinless eyes
That loved him but in holy girlish wise
For noble joy in his fair manliness
And trust and tender wonder; none the less
She thought if God had given her grace to be
Man, and make war on danger of earth and sea,
Even such a man she would be; for his stroke
Was mightiest as the mightier water broke,
And in sheer measure like strong music drave
Clean through the wet weight of the wallowing wave;
And as a tune before a great king played
For triumph was the tune their strong strokes made,
And sped the ship through with smooth strife of oars
Over the mid sea's grey foam-paven floors,
For all the loud breach of the waves at will.
So for an hour they fought the storm out still,
And the shorn foam spun from the blades, and high
The keel sprang from the wave-ridge, and the sky
Glared at them for a breath's space through the rain;
Then the bows with a sharp shock plunged again
Down, and the sea clashed on them, and so rose
The bright stem like one panting from swift blows,
And as a swimmer's joyous beaten head
Rears itself laughing, so in that sharp stead
The light ship lifted her long quivering bows
As might the man his buffeted strong brows
Out of the wave-breach; for with one stroke yet
Went all men's oars together, strongly set
As to loud music, and with hearts uplift
They smote their strong way through the drench and drift:

Till the keen hour had chafed itself to death
And the east wind fell fitfully, breath by breath,
Tired; and across the thin and slackening rain
Sprang the face southward of the sun again.
Then all they rested and were eased at heart.

Atalanta in Calydon

THE ARGUMENT

Althæa, daughter of Thestius and Eurythemis, queen of Calydon, being with child of Meleager her first-born son, dreamed that she brought forth a brand burning; and upon his birth came the three Fates and prophesied of him three things, namely these; that he should have great strength of his hands, and good fortune in this life, and that he should live no longer when the brand then in the fire were consumed: wherefore his mother plucked it forth and kept it by her. And the child being a man grown sailed with Jason after the fleece of gold, and won himself great praise of all men living; and when the tribes of the north and west made war upon Ætolia, he fought against their army and scattered it. But Artemis, having at the first stirred up these tribes to war against Œneus king of Calydon, because he had offered sacrifice to all the gods saving her alone, but her he had forgotten to honour, was yet more wroth because of the destruction of this army, and sent upon the land of Calydon a wild boar which slew many and wasted all their increase, but him could none slay, and many went against him and perished. Then were all the chief men of Greece gathered together, and among them Atalanta daughter of Iasius the Arcadian, a virgin; for whose sake Artemis let slay the boar, seeing she favoured the maiden greatly; and Meleager having despatched it gave the spoil thereof to Atalanta, as one beyond measure enamoured of her; but the brethren of Althæa his mother, Toxeus and Plexippus, with such others as misliked that she only should bear off the praise whereas many had borne the labour, laid wait for her to take away her spoil; but Meleager fought against them and slew them: whom when Althæa their sister beheld and knew to be slain of her son, she waxed for wrath and sorrow like as one mad, and taking the brand whereby the measure of her son's life was meted to him, she cast it upon a fire; and with the wasting thereof his life likewise wasted away, that being brought back to his father's house he died in a brief space; and his mother also endured not long after for very sorrow; and this was his end, and the end of that hunting.

CHORUS

When the hounds of spring are on winter's traces,
  The mother of months in meadow or plain
Fills the shadows and windy places
  With lisp of leaves and ripple of rain;
And the brown bright nightingale amorous
Is half assuaged for Itylus,
For the Thracian ships and the foreign faces,
  The tongueless vigil, and all the pain.

Come with bows bent and with emptying of quivers,
  Maiden most perfect, lady of light,
With a noise of winds and many rivers,
  With a clamour of waters, and with might;
Bind on thy sandals, O thou most fleet,
Over the splendour and speed of thy feet;
For the faint east quickens, the wan west shivers,
  Round the feet of the day and the feet of the night.

Where shall we find her, how shall we sing to her,
  Fold our hands round her knees, and cling?
O that man's heart were as fire and could spring to her,
  Fire, or the strength of the streams that spring!
For the stars and the winds are unto her
As raiment, as songs of the harp-player;
For the risen stars and the fallen cling to her,
  And the southwest-wind and the west-wind sing.

For winter's rains and ruins are over,
  And all the season of snows and sins;
The days dividing lover and lover,
  The light that loses, the night that wins;
And time remembered is grief forgotten,
And frosts are slain and flowers begotten,
And in green underwood and cover
  Blossom by blossom the spring begins.

The full streams feed on flower of rushes,
  Ripe grasses trammel a travelling foot,
The faint fresh flame of the young year flushes
  From leaf to flower and flower to fruit;
And fruit and leaf are as gold and fire,
And the oat is heard above the lyre,
And the hoofèd heel of a satyr crushes
  The chestnut-husk at the chestnut-root.

And Pan by noon and Bacchus by night,
  Fleeter of foot than the fleet-foot kid,
Follows with dancing and fills with delight
  The Mænad and the Bassarid;
And soft as lips that laugh and hide
The laughing leaves of the trees divide,
And screen from seeing and leave in sight
  The god pursuing, the maiden hid.

The ivy falls with the Bacchanal's hair
   Over her eyebrows hiding her eyes;
The wild vine slipping down leaves bare
   Her bright breast shortening into sighs;
The wild vine slips with the weight of its leaves,
But the berried ivy catches and cleaves
To the limbs that glitter, the feet that scare
   The wolf that follows, the fawn that flies.

* * * * * *

ALTHÆA

So light a thing was this man, grown so great
Men cast their heads back, seeing against the sun
Blaze the armed man carven on his shield, and hear
The laughter of little bells along the brace
Ring, as birds singing or flutes blown, and watch,
High up, the cloven shadow of either plume
Divide the bright light of the brass, and make
His helmet as a windy and wintering moon
Seen through blown cloud and plume-like drift, when ships
Drive, and men strive with all the sea, and oars
Break, and the beaks dip under, drinking death.

* * * * * *

CHORUS

Before the beginning of years
   There came to the making of man
Time, with a gift of tears;
   Grief, with a glass that ran;
Pleasure, with pain for leaven;
   Summer, with flowers that fell;
Remembrance fallen from heaven,
   And madness risen from hell;
Strength without hands to smite;
   Love that endures for a breath:

Night, the shadow of light,
  And life, the shadow of death.
And the high gods took in hand
  Fire, and the falling of tears,
And a measure of sliding sand
  From under the feet of the years;
And froth and drift of the sea;
  And dust of the labouring earth;
And bodies of things to be
  In the houses of death and of birth;
And wrought with weeping and laughter,
  And fashioned with loathing and love
With life before and after
  And death beneath and above,
For a day and a night and a morrow,
  That his strength might endure for a span
With travail and heavy sorrow,
  The holy spirit of man.

From the winds of the north and the south
  They gathered as unto strife;
They breathed upon his mouth,
  They filled his body with life;
Eyesight and speech they wrought
  For the veils of the soul therein,
A time for labour and thought,
  A time to serve and to sin;
They gave him light in his ways,
  And love, and a space for delight,
And beauty and length of days,
  And night, and sleep in the night.
His speech is a burning fire;
  With his lips he travaileth;

In his heart is a blind desire,
  In his eyes foreknowledge of death;
He weaves, and is clothed with derision;
  Sows, and he shall not reap;
His life is a watch or a vision
  Between a sleep and a sleep.

* * * * * *

ALTHÆA TO MELEAGER

But thou, son, be not filled with evil dreams,
Nor with desire of these things; for with time
Blind love burns out; but if one feed it full
Till some discolouring stain dyes all his life,
He shall keep nothing praiseworthy, nor die
The sweet wise death of old men honourable,
Who have lived out all the length of all their years
Blameless, and seen well-pleased the face of gods,
And without shame and without fear have wrought
Things memorable, and while their days held out
In sight of all men and the sun's great light
Have gat them glory and given of their own praise
To the earth that bare them and the day that bred,
Home friends and far-off hospitalities,
And filled with gracious and memorial fame
Lands loved of summer or washed by violent seas,
Towns populous and many unfooted ways,
And alien lips and native with their own.
But when white age and venerable death
Mow down the strength and life within their limbs,
Drain out the blood and darken their clear eyes,
Immortal honour is on them, having past
Through splendid life and death desirable
To the clear seat and remote throne of souls,
Lands indiscoverable in the unheard-of west,

Round which the strong stream of a sacred sea
Rolls without wind for ever, and the snow
There shows not her white wings and windy feet,
Nor thunder nor swift rain saith anything,
Nor the sun burns, but all things rest and thrive;
And these, filled full of days, divine and dead,
Sages and singers fiery from the god,
And such as loved their land and all things good
And, best beloved of best men, liberty,
Free lives and lips, free hands of men free-born,
And whatsoever on earth was honourable
And whosoever of all the ephemeral seed,
Live there a life no liker to the gods
But nearer than their life of terrene days.
Love thou such life and look for such a death.
But from the light and fiery dreams of love
Spring heavy sorrows and a sleepless life,
Visions not dreams, whose lids no charm shall close
Nor song assuage them waking; and swift death
Crushes with sterile feet the unripening ear,
Treads out the timeless vintage; whom do thou
Eschewing embrace the luck of this thy life,
Not without honour; and it shall bear to thee
Such fruit as men reap from spent hours and wear,
Few men, but happy; of whom be thou, O son,
Happiest, if thou submit thy soul to fate,
And set thine eyes and heart on hopes high-born
And divine deeds and abstinence divine.
So shalt thou be toward all men all thy days
As light and might communicable, and burn
From heaven among the stars above the hours,
And break not as a man breaks nor burn down:
For to whom other of all heroic names
Have the gods given his life in hand as thine?

And gloriously hast thou lived, and made thy life
To me that bare thee and to all men born
Thankworthy, a praise for ever; and hast won fame
When wild wars broke all round thy father's house,
And the mad people of windy mountain ways
Laid spears against us like a sea, and all
Ætolia thundered with Thessalian hoofs;
Yet these, as wind baffles the foam, and beats
Straight back the relaxed ripple, didst thou break
And loosen all their lances, till undone
And man from man they fell.

* * * * * *

MELEAGER TO ALTHÆA

O mother, I am not fain to strive in speech
Nor set my mouth against thee, who art wise
Even as they say and full of sacred words.
But one thing I know surely, and cleave to this;
That though I be not subtle of wit as thou
Nor womanlike to weave sweet words, and melt
Mutable minds of wise men as with fire,
I too, doing justly and reverencing the gods,
Shall not want wit to see what things be right.
For whom they love and whom reject, being gods,
There is no man but seeth, and in good time
Submits himself, refraining all his heart.
And I too as thou sayest have seen great things;
Seen otherwhere, but chiefly when the sail
First caught between stretched ropes the roaring west,
And all our oars smote eastward, and the wind
First flung round faces of seafaring men
White splendid snow-flakes of the sundering foam,
And the first furrow in virginal green sea
Followed the plunging ploughshare of hewn pine,
And closed, as when deep sleep subdues man's breath

Lips close and heart subsides; and closing, shone
Sunlike with many a Nereid's hair, and moved
Round many a trembling mouth of doubtful gods,
Risen out of sunless and sonorous gulfs
Through waning water and into shallow light,
That watched us; and when flying the dove was snared
As with men's hands, but we shot after and sped
Clear through the irremeable Symplegades;
And chiefliest when hoar beach and herbless cliff
Stood out ahead from Colchis, and we heard
Clefts hoarse with wind, and saw through narrowing reefs
The lightning of the intolerable wave
Flash, and the white wet flame of breakers burn
Far under a kindling south-wind, as a lamp
Burns and bends all its blowing flame one way;
Wild heights untravelled of the wind, and vales
Cloven seaward by their violent streams, and white
With bitter flowers and bright salt scurf of brine;
Heard sweep their sharp swift gales, and bowing birdwise
Shriek with birds' voices, and with furious feet
Tread loose the long skirts of a storm; and saw
The whole white Euxine clash together and fall
Full-mouthed, and thunderous from a thousand throats:
Yet we drew thither and won the fleece and won
Medea, deadlier than the sea.

* * * * * *

ALTHÆA TO MELEAGER

For there was never a mother woman-born
Loved her sons better; and never a queen of men
More perfect in her heart toward whom she loved.
For what lies light on many and they forget,
Small things and transitory as a wind o' the sea,
I forget never; I have seen thee all thine years
A man in arms, strong and a joy to men

Seeing thine head glitter and thine hand burn its way
Through a heavy and iron furrow of sundering spears;
But always also a flower of three suns old,
The small one thing that lying drew down my life
To lie with thee and feed thee; a child and weak,
Mine, a delight to no man, sweet to me.
Who then sought to thee? who gat help? who knew
If thou wert goodly? nay, no man at all.
Or what sea saw thee, or sounded with thine oar,
Child? or what strange land shone with war through thee?
But fair for me thou wert, O little life,
Fruitless, the fruit of mine own flesh, and blind,
More than much gold, ungrown, a foolish flower.
For silver nor bright snow nor feather of foam
Was whiter, and no gold yellower than thine hair,
O child, my child; and now thou art lordlier grown,
Not lovelier, nor a new thing in mine eyes,
I charge thee by thy soul and this my breast,
Fear thou the gods and me and thine own heart,
Lest all these turn against thee; for who knows
What wind upon what wave of altering time
Shall speak a storm and blow calamity?
And there is nothing stabile in the world
But the gods break it; yet not less, fair son,
If but one thing be stronger, if one endure,
Surely the bitter and the rooted love
That burns between us, going from me to thee,
Shall more endure than all things. What dost thou,
Following strange loves? why wilt thou kill mine heart?
Lo, I talk wild and windy words, and fall
From my clear wits, and seem of mine own self
Dethroned, dispraised, disseated; and my mind,
That was my crown, breaks, and mine heart is gone,
And I am naked of my soul, and stand

Ashamed, as a mean woman; take thou thought:
Live if thou wilt, and if thou wilt not, look,
The gods have given thee life to lose or keep,
Thou shalt not die as men die, but thine end
Fallen upon thee shall break me unaware.

MELEAGER

Queen, my whole heart is molten with thy tears,
And my limbs yearn with pity of thee, and love
Compels with grief mine eyes and labouring breath;
For what thou art I know thee, and this thy breast
And thy fair eyes I worship, and am bound
Toward thee in spirit and love thee in all my soul.
For there is nothing terribler to men
Than the sweet face of mothers, and the might.
But what shall be let be; for us the day
Once only lives a little, and is not found.
Time and the fruitful hour are more than we,
And these lay hold upon us; but thou, God,
Zeus, the sole steersman of the helm of things,
Father, be swift to see us, and as thou wilt
Help: or if adverse, as thou wilt, refrain.

* * * * * *

ATALANTA

I am not mighty-minded, nor desire
Crowns, nor the spoil of slain things nor the fame;
Feed ye on these, eat and wax fat; cry out,
Laugh, having eaten, and leap without a lyre,
Sing, mix the wind with clamour, smite and shake
Sonorous timbrels and tumultuous hair,
And fill the dance up with tempestuous feet,
For I will none; but having prayed my prayers
And made thank-offering for prosperities,
I shall go hence and no man see me more.

* * * * * *

HERALD

But Meleager, but thy son,
Right in the wild way of the coming curse
Rock-rooted, fair with fierce and fastened lips,
Clear eyes, and springing muscle and shortening limb—
With chin aslant indrawn to a tightening throat,
Grave, and with gathered sinews, like a god,—
Aimed on the left side his well-handled spear
Grasped where the ash was knottiest hewn, and smote,
And with no missile wound, the monstrous boar
Right in the hairiest hollow of his hide
Under the last rib, sheer through bulk and bone,
Deep in; and deeply smitten, and to death,
The heavy horror with his hanging shafts
Leapt, and fell furiously, and from raging lips
Foamed out the latest wrath of all his life.

* * * * * *

MELEAGER

Let your hands meet
Round the weight of my head;
Lift ye my feet
As the feet of the dead;
For the flesh of my body is molten, the limbs of it molten as lead.

CHORUS

O thy luminous face!
Thine imperious eyes!
O the grief, O the grace,
As of day when it dies!
Who is this bending over thee, lord, with tears and suppression of sighs?

MELEAGER

Is a bride so fair?
Is a maid so meek?
With unchapleted hair,
With unfilleted cheek,
Atalanta, the pure among women, whose name is as blessing to speak.

ATALANTA

I would that with feet
Unsandalled, unshod,
Overbold, overfleet,
I had swum not nor trod
From Arcadia to Calydon northward, a blast of the envy of God.

MELEAGER

Unto each man his fate;
Unto each as he saith
In whose fingers the weight
Of the world is as breath;
Yet I would that in clamour of battle mine hands had laid hold upon death.

CHORUS

Not with cleaving of shields
And their clash in thine ear,
When the lord of fought fields
Breaketh spearshaft from spear,
Thou art broken, our Lord, thou art broken, with travail and labour and fear.

MELEAGER

Would God he had found me
Beneath fresh boughs!
Would God he had bound me
Unawares in mine house,
With light in mine eyes, and songs in my lips, and a crown on my brows!

CHORUS

Whence art thou sent from us?
Whither thy goal?
How art thou rent from us,
Thou that wert whole,
As with severing of eyelids and eyes, as with sundering of body and soul!

MELEAGER

My heart is within me
As an ash in the fire;
Whosoever hath seen me,
Without lute, without lyre,
Shall sing of me grievous things, even things that were ill to desire.

CHORUS

Who shall raise thee
From the house of the dead?
Or what man praise thee
That thy praise may be said?
Alas thy beauty! alas thy body! alas thine head!

* * * * * *

MELEAGER

For the dead man no home is;
Ah, better to be
What the flower of the foam is
In fields of the sea,
That the sea-waves might be as my raiment, the gulf-stream a garment for me.

CHORUS

Who shall seek thee and bring
And restore thee thy day,
When the dove dipt her wing
And the oars won their way
Where the narrowing Symplegades whitened the straits of Propontis with spray?

MELEAGER

Will ye crown me my tomb
Or exalt me my name,
Now my spirits consume,
Now my flesh is a flame?
Let the sea slake it once, and men speak of me sleeping to praise me or shame.

By the North Sea

...The delight that he[1] takes but in living
Is more than of all things that live:
For the world that has all things for giving
Has nothing so goodly to give:
But more than delight his desire is,
For the goal where his pinions would be
Is immortal as air or as fire is,
Immense as the sea.

[1] The Wind.

Though hence come the moan that he borrows
From darkness and depth of the night,
Though hence be the spring of his sorrows,
Hence too is the joy of his might;
The delight that his doom is for ever
To seek and desire and rejoice,
And the sense that eternity never
Shall silence his voice.

That satiety never may stifle
Nor weariness ever estrange
Nor time be so strong as to rifle
Nor change be so great as to change
His gift that renews in the giving,
The joy that exalts him to be
Alone of all elements living
The lord of the sea.

What is fire, that its flame should consume her[1]?
More fierce than all fires are her waves:
What is earth, that its gulfs should entomb her?
More deep are her own than their graves.
Life shrinks from his pinions that cover
The darkness by thunders bedinned:
But she knows him, her lord and her lover
The godhead of wind.

For a season his wings are about her,
His breath on her lips for a space;
Such rapture he wins not without her
In the width of his worldwide race.
Though the forests bow down, and the mountains
Wax dark, and the tribes of them flee,
His delight is more deep in the fountains
And springs of the sea.

[1] The Sea.

There are those too of mortals that love him,
  There are souls that desire and require,
Be the glories of midnight above him
  Or beneath him the daysprings of fire:
And their hearts are as harps that approve him
  And praise him as chords of a lyre
That were fain with their music to move him
      To meet their desire

To descend through the darkness to grace them,
  Till darkness were lovelier than light:
To encompass and grasp and embrace them,
  Till their weakness were one with his might:
With the strength of his wings to caress them,
  With the blast of his breath to set free;
With the mouths of his thunders to bless them
      For sons of the sea.

For these have the toil and the guerdon
  That the wind has eternally: these
Have part in the boon and the burden
  Of the sleepless unsatisfied breeze,
That finds not, but seeking rejoices
  That possession can work him no wrong:
And the voice at the heart of their voice is
      The sense of his song.

For the wind's is their doom and their blessing;
  To desire, and have always above
A possession beyond their possessing,
  A love beyond reach of their love.
Green earth has her sons and her daughters,
  And these have their guerdons; but we
Are the wind's and the sun's and the water's,
      Elect of the sea.

Adieux à Marie Stuart

I

Queen, for whose house my fathers fought,
    With hopes that rose and fell,
Red star of boyhood's fiery thought,
    Farewell.

They gave their lives, and I, my queen,
    Have given you of my life,
Seeing your brave star burn high between
    Men's strife.

The strife that lightened round their spears
    Long since fell still: so long
Hardly may hope to last in years
    My song.

But still through strife of time and thought
    Your light on me too fell:
Queen, in whose name we sang or fought,
    Farewell.

II

There beats no heart on either border
    Wherethrough the north blasts blow
But keeps your memory as a warder
    His beacon-fire aglow.

Long since it fired with love and wonder
    Mine, for whose April age
Blithe midsummer made banquet under
    The shade of Hermitage.

Soft sang the burn's blithe notes, that gather
    Strength to ring true:
And air and trees and sun and heather
    Remembered you.

Old border ghosts of fight or fairy
Or love or teen,
These they forgot, remembering Mary
The Queen.

III

Queen once of Scots and ever of ours
Whose sires brought forth for you
Their lives to strew your way like flowers,
Adieu.

Dead is full many a dead man's name
Who died for you this long
Time past: shall this too fare the same,
My song?

But surely, though it die or live,
Your face was worth
All that a man may think to give
On earth.

No darkness cast of years between
Can darken you:
Man's love will never bid my queen
Adieu.

IV

Love hangs like light about your name
As music round the shell:
No heart can take of you a tame
Farewell.

Yet, when your very face was seen,
Ill gifts were yours for giving:
Love gat strange guerdons of my queen
When living.

O diamond heart unflawed and clear,
The whole world's crowning jewel!
Was ever heart so deadly dear
So cruel?

Yet none for you of all that bled
Grudged once one drop that fell:
Not one to life reluctant said
Farewell.

V

Strange love they have given you, love disloyal,
Who mock with praise your name,
To leave a head so rare and royal
Too low for praise or blame.

You could not love nor hate, they tell us,
You had nor sense nor sting:
In God's name, then, what plague befell us
To fight for such a thing?

"Some faults the gods will give," to fetter
Man's highest intent:
But surely you were something better
Than innocent!

No maid that strays with steps unwary
Through snares unseen,
But one to live and die for; Mary,
The Queen.

VI

Forgive them all their praise, who blot
Your fame with praise of you:
Then love may say, and falter not,
Adieu.

Yet some you hardly would forgive
Who did you much less wrong
Once: but resentment should not live
Too long.

They never saw your lip's bright bow,
Your swordbright eyes,
The bluest of heavenly things below
The skies.

Clear eyes that love's self finds most like
A swordblade's blue,
A swordblade's ever keen to strike,
Adieu.

VII

Though all things breathe or sound of fight
That yet make up your spell,
To bid you were to bid the light
Farewell.

Farewell the song says only, being
A star whose race is run:
Farewell the soul says never, seeing
The sun.

Yet, wellnigh as with flash of tears,
The song must say but so
That took your praise up twenty years
Ago.

More bright than stars or moons that vary,
Sun kindling heaven and hell,
Here, after all these years, Queen Mary,
Farewell.

A Child's Laughter

All the bells of heaven may ring,
All the birds of heaven may sing,
All the wells on earth may spring,
All the winds on earth may bring
  All sweet sounds together;
Sweeter far than all things heard,
Hand of harper, tone of bird,
Sound of woods at sundawn stirred,
Welling water's winsome word,
  Wind in warm wan weather,

One thing yet there is, that none
Hearing ere its chime be done
Knows not well the sweetest one
Heard of man beneath the sun,
  Hoped in heaven hereafter;
Soft and strong and loud and light,
Very sound of very light
Heard from morning's rosiest height,
When the soul of all delight
  Fills a child's clear laughter.

Golden bells of welcome rolled
Never forth such notes, nor told
Hours so blithe in tones so bold,
As the radiant mouth of gold
  Here that rings forth heaven.
If the golden-crested wren
Were a nightingale—why, then,
Something seen and heard of men
Might be half as sweet as when
  Laughs a child of seven.

Nephelidia

From the depth of the dreamy decline of the dawn through a notable nimbus of nebulous noonshine,
Pallid and pink as the palm of the flag-flower that flickers with fear of the flies as they float,
Are they looks of our lovers that lustrously lean from a marvel of mystic miraculous moonshine,
These that we feel in the blood of our blushes that thicken and threaten with throbs through the throat?
Thicken and thrill as a theatre thronged at appeal of an actor's appalled agitation,
Fainter with fear of the fires of the future than pale with the promise of pride in the past;
Flushed with the famishing fullness of fever that reddens with radiance of rathe recreation,
Gaunt as the ghastliest of glimpses that gleam through the gloom of the gloaming when ghosts go aghast?
Nay, for the nick of the tick of the time is a tremulous touch on the temples of terror,
Strained as the sinews yet strenuous with strife of the dead who is dumb as the dust-heaps of death:
Surely no soul is it, sweet as the spasm of erotic emotional exquisite error,
Bathed in the balms of beatified bliss, beatific itself by beatitude's breath.
Surely no spirit or sense of a soul that was soft to the spirit and soul of our senses
Sweetens the stress of suspiring suspicion that sobs in the semblance and sound of a sigh;
Only this oracle opens Olympian, in mystical moods and triangular tenses—
"Life is the lust of a lamp for the light that is dark till the dawn of the day when we die."

Mild is the mirk and monotonous music of memory, melodiously mute as it may be,
While the hope in the heart of a hero is bruised by the breach of men's rapiers, resigned to the rod;
Made meek as a mother whose bosom-beats bound with the bliss-bringing bulk of a balm-breathing baby,
As they grope through the grave-yard of creeds, under skies growing green at a groan for the grimness of God.
Blank is the book of his bounty beholden of old, and its binding is blacker than bluer:
Out of blue into black is the scheme of the skies, and their dews are the wine of the bloodshed of things;
Till the darkling desire of delight shall be free as a fawn that is freed from the fangs that pursue her,
Till the heart-beats of hell shall be hushed by a hymn from the hunt that has harried the kennel of kings.

On a Country Road

Along these low pleached lanes, on such a day,
So soft a day as this, through shade and sun,
With glad grave eyes that scanned the glad wild way,
And heart still hovering o'er a song begun,
And smile that warmed the world with benison,
Our father, lord long since of lordly rhyme,
Long since hath haply ridden, when the lime
Bloomed broad above him, flowering where he came.
Because thy passage once made warm this clime,
Our father Chaucer, here we praise thy name.

Each year that England clothes herself with May,
She takes thy likeness on her. Time hath spun
Fresh raiment all in vain and strange array
For earth and man's new spirit, fain to shun
Things past for dreams of better to be won,

Through many a century since thy funeral chime
Rang, and men deemed it death's most direful crime
To have spared not thee for very love or shame;
And yet, while mists round last year's memories climb,
Our father Chaucer, here we praise thy name.

Each turn of the old wild road whereon we stray,
Meseems, might bring us face to face with one
Whom seeing we could not but give thanks, and pray
For England's love our father and her son
To speak with us as once in days long done
With all men, sage and churl and monk and mime,
Who knew not as we know the soul sublime
That sang for song's love more than lust of fame.
Yet, though this be not, yet, in happy time,
Our father Chaucer, here we praise thy name.

Friend, even as bees about the flowering thyme,
Years crowd on years, till hoar decay begrime
Names once beloved; but, seeing the sun the same,
As birds of autumn fain to praise the prime,
Our father Chaucer, here we praise thy name.

A Swimmer's Dream

. . . A dream, a dream is it all—the season,
The sky, the water, the wind, the shore?
A day-born dream of divine unreason,
A marvel moulded of sleep—no more?
For the cloudlike wave that my limbs while cleaving
Feel as in slumber beneath them heaving
Soothes the sense as to slumber, leaving
Sense of nought that was known of yore.

A purer passion, a lordlier leisure,
  A peace more happy than lives on land,
Fulfils with pulse of diviner pleasure
  The dreaming head and the steering hand.
I lean my cheek to the cold grey pillow,
The deep soft swell of the full broad billow,
And close mine eyes for delight past measure,
  And wish the wheel of the world would stand.

The wild-winged hour that we fain would capture
  Falls as from heaven that its light feet clomb,
So brief, so soft, and so full the rapture
  Was felt that soothed me with sense of home.
To sleep, to swim, and to dream, for ever—
Such joy the vision of man saw never;
For here too soon will a dark day sever
  The sea-bird's wing from the sea-wave's foam.

A dream, and more than a dream, and dimmer
  At once and brighter than dreams that flee,
The moment's joy of the seaward swimmer
  Abides, remembered as truth may be.
Not all the joy and not all the glory
Must fade as leaves when the woods wax hoary;
For there the downs and the sea-banks glimmer,
  And here to south of them swells the sea.

Eton: An Ode

FOR THE FOUR HUNDRED AND FIFTIETH ANNIVERSARY OF THE FOUNDATION OF THE COLLEGE

I

Four hundred summers and fifty have shone on the meadows of Thames and died
Since Eton arose in an age that was darkness, and shone by his radiant side
As a star that the spell of a wise man's word bade live and ascend and abide.

And ever as time's flow brightened, a river more dark than the storm-clothed sea,
And age upon age rose fairer and larger in promise of hope set free,
With England Eton her child kept pace as a fostress of men to be.

And ever as earth waxed wiser, and softer the beating of time's wide wings,
Since fate fell dark on her father, most hapless and gentlest of star-crossed kings,
Her praise has increased as the chant of the dawn that the choir of the noon outsings.

II

Storm and cloud in the skies were loud, and lightning mocked at the blind sun's light;
War and woe on the land below shed heavier shadow than falls from night;
Dark was earth at her dawn of birth as here her record of praise is bright.

Clear and fair through her morning air the light first laugh of the sunlit stage
Rose and rang as a fount that sprang from depths yet dark with a spent storm's rage,
Loud and glad as a boy's, and bade the sunrise open on Shakespeare's age.

Lords of state and of war, whom fate found strong in battle, in counsel strong,
Here, ere fate had approved them great, abode their season, and thought not long:
Here too first was the lark's note nursed that filled and flooded the skies with song.

III

Shelley, lyric lord of England's lordliest singers, here first heard
Ring from lips of poets crowned and dead the Promethean word
Whence his soul took fire, and power to outsoar the sunward-soaring bird.

Still the reaches of the river, still the light on field and hill,
Still the memories held aloft as lamps for hope's young fire to fill,
Shine, and while the light of England lives shall shine for England still.

When four hundred more and fifty years have risen and shone and set,
Bright with names that men remember, loud with names that men forget,
Haply here shall Eton's record be what England finds it yet.

Jacobite Song

Now who will speak, and lie not,
And pledge not life, but give?
Slaves herd with herded cattle:
The dawn grows bright for battle
And if we die, we die not;
And if we live, we live.

The faith our fathers fought for,
The kings our fathers knew,
We fight but as they fought for:
We seek the goal they sought for,
The chance they hailed and knew,
The praise they strove and wrought for,
To leave their blood as dew
On fields that flower anew.

Men live that serve the stranger;
Hounds live that huntsmen tame:
These life-days of our living
Are days of God's good giving
Where death smiles soft on danger
And life scowls dark on shame.

And what would you do other,
Sweet wife, if you were I?
And how should you be other,
My sister, than your brother,
If you were man as I,
Born of our sire and mother,
With choice to cower and fly,
And chance to strike and die?

No churl's our oldworld name is,
The lands we leave are fair:

But fairer far than these are,
But wide as all the seas are,
But high as heaven the fame is
  That if we die we share.

Our name the night may swallow,
  Our lands the churl may take:
But night nor death may swallow,
Nor hell's nor heaven's dim hollow,
  The star whose height we take,
The star whose light we follow
  For faith's unfaltering sake
  Till hope that sleeps awake.

Soft hope's light lure we serve not,
  Nor follow, fain to find:
Dark time's last word may smite her
Dead, ere man's falsehood blight her:
But though she die, we swerve not,
  Who cast not eye behind.

Faith speaks when hope dissembles:
  Faith lives when hope lies dead:
If death as life dissembles,
And all that night assembles
  Of stars at dawn lie dead,
Faint hope that smiles and trembles
  May tell not well for dread:
  But faith has heard it said.

Now who will fight, and fly not,
  And grudge not life to give?
And who will strike beside us,
If life's or death's light guide us?
For if we live, we die not,
  And if we die, we live.

A Channel Passage

1855

Forth from Calais, at dawn of night, when sunset summer on autumn shone,
Fared the steamer alert and loud through seas whence only the sun was gone:
Soft and sweet as the sky they smiled, and bade man welcome: a dim sweet hour
Gleamed and whispered in wind and sea, and heaven was fair as a field in flower.
Stars fulfilled the desire of the darkling world as with music: the starbright air
Made the face of the sea, if aught may make the face of the sea, more fair.

Whence came change? Was the sweet night weary of rest? What anguish awoke in the dark?
Sudden, sublime, the strong storm spake: we heard the thunders as hounds that bark.
Lovelier if aught may be lovelier than stars, we saw the lightnings exalt the sky,
Living and lustrous and rapturous as love that is born but to quicken and lighten and die.
Heaven's own heart at its highest of delight found utterance in music and semblance in fire:
Thunder on thunder exulted, rejoicing to live and to satiate the night's desire.

And the night was alive and anhungered of life as a tiger from toils cast free:
And a rapture of rage made joyous the spirit and strength of the soul of the sea.

All the weight of the wind bore down on it, freighted with death for fraught:
And the keen waves kindled and quickened as things transfigured or things distraught.
And madness fell on them laughing and leaping; and madness came on the wind:
And the might and the light and the darkness of storm were as storm in the heart of Ind.
Such glory, such terror, such passion, as lighten and harrow the far fierce East,
Rang, shone, spake, shuddered around us: the night was an altar with death for priest.
The channel that sunders England from shores where never was man born free
Was clothed with the likeness and thrilled with the strength and the wrath of a tropic sea.
As a wild steed ramps in rebellion, and rears till it swerves from a backward fall,
The strong ship struggled and reared, and her deck was upright as a sheer cliff's wall.
Stern and prow plunged under, alternate: a glimpse, a recoil, a breath,
And she sprang as the life in a god made man would spring at the throat of death.
Three glad hours, and it seemed not an hour of supreme and supernal joy,
Filled full with delight that revives in remembrance a sea-bird's heart in a boy.
For the central crest of the night was cloud that thundered and flamed, sublime
As the splendour and song of the soul everlasting that quickens the pulse of time.
The glory beholden of man in a vision, the music of light overheard,

The rapture and radiance of battle, the life that abides in the fire of a word,
In the midmost heaven enkindled, was manifest far on the face of the sea,
And the rage in the roar of the voice of the waters was heard but when heaven breathed free.
Far eastward, clear of the covering of cloud, the sky laughed out into light
From the rims of the storm to the sea's dark edge with flames that were flowerlike and white.
The leaping and luminous blossoms of live sheet lightning that laugh as they fade
From the cloud's black base to the black wave's brim rejoiced in the light they made.
Far westward, throned in a silent sky, where life was in lustrous tune,
Shone, sweeter and surer than morning or evening, the steadfast smile of the moon.
The limitless heaven that enshrined them was lovelier than dreams may behold, and deep
As life or as death, revealed and transfigured, may shine on the soul through sleep.
All glories of toil and of triumph and passion and pride that it yearns to know
Bore witness there to the soul of its likeness and kinship, above and below.
The joys of the lightnings, the songs of the thunders, the strong sea's labour and rage,
Were tokens and signs of the war that is life and is joy for the soul to wage.
No thought strikes deeper or higher than the heights and the depths that the night made bare,
Illimitable, infinite, awful and joyful, alive in the summit of air—

Air stilled and thrilled by the tempest that thundered between its reign and the sea's,
Rebellious, rapturous, and transient as faith or as terror that bows men's knees.
No love sees loftier and fairer the form of its godlike vision in dreams
Than the world shone then, when the sky and the sea were as love for a breath's length seems—
One utterly, mingled and mastering and mastered and laughing with love that subsides
As the glad mad night sank panting and satiate with storm, and released the tides.
In the dense mid channel the steam-souled ship hung hovering, assailed and withheld
As a soul born royal, if life or if death be against it, is thwarted and quelled.
As the glories of myriads of glowworms in lustrous grass on a boundless lawn
Were the glories of flames phosphoric that made of the water a light like dawn.
A thousand Phosphors, a thousand Hespers, awoke in the churning sea,
And the swift soft hiss of them living and dying was clear as a tune could be;
As a tune that is played by the fingers of death on the keys of life or of sleep,
Audible alway alive in the storm, too fleet for a dream to keep:
Too fleet, too sweet for a dream to recover and thought to remember awake:
Light subtler and swifter than lightning, that whispers and laughs in the live storm's wake,
In the wild bright wake of the storm, in the dense loud heart of the labouring hour,

A harvest of stars by the storm's hand reaped, each fair as a
star-shaped flower.
And sudden and soft as the passing of sleep is the passing of
tempest seemed
When the light and the sound of it sank, and the glory was
gone as a dream half dreamed.
The glory, the terror, the passion that made of the midnight
a miracle, died,
Not slain at a stroke, nor in gradual reluctance abated of
power and of pride;
With strong swift subsidence, awful as power that is wearied
of power upon earth,
As a God that were wearied of power upon heaven, and
were fain of a new God's birth,
The might of the night subsided: the tyranny kindled in
darkness fell:
And the sea and the sky put off them the rapture and
radiance of heaven and of hell.
The waters, heaving and hungering at heart, made way,
and were wellnigh fain,
For the ship that had fought them, and wrestled, and
revelled in labour, to cease from her pain.
And an end was made of it: only remembrance endures of
the glad loud strife;
And the sense that a rapture so royal may come not again
in the passage of life.

Review of *L'Homme qui rit*

Once only in my life I have seen the likeness of Victor Hugo's genius. Crossing over when a boy from Ostend, I had the fortune to be caught in midchannel by a thunderstorm strong enough to delay the packet some three good hours over the due time. About midnight the thundercloud was right overhead, full of incessant sound and fire, lightening and darkening so rapidly that it seemed to have life, and a delight in its life. At the same hour the sky was clear to the west, and all along the sea-line there sprang and sank as to music a restless dance or chase of summer lightnings across the lower sky: a race and riot of lights, beautiful and rapid as a course of shining Oceanides along the tremulous floor of the sea. Eastward at the same moment the space of clear sky was higher and wider, a splendid semicircle of too intense purity to be called blue; it was of no colour nameable by man; and midway in it between the storm and the sea hung the motionless full moon; Artemis watching with a serene splendour of scorn the battle of Titans and the revel of nymphs, from her stainless and Olympian summit of divine and indifferent light. Underneath and about us the sea was paved with flame; the whole water trembled and hissed with phosphoric fire; even through the wind and thunder I could hear the crackling and sputtering of the water-sparks. In the same heaven and in the same hour there shone at once the three contrasted glories, golden and fiery and white, of moonlight and of the double lightnings, forked and sheet; and under all this miraculous heaven lay a flaming floor of water.

That, in a most close and exact symbol, is the best possible definition I can give of Victor Hugo's genius....

Byron

. . . Between *Childe Harold* and *Don Juan* the same difference exists which a swimmer feels between lake-water and sea-water: the one is fluent, yielding, invariable; the other has in it a life and pulse, a sting and a swell, which touch and excite the nerves like fire or like music. Across the stanzas of *Don Juan* we swim forward as over "the broad backs of the sea"; they break and glitter, hiss and laugh, murmur and move, like waves that sound or that subside. There is in them a delicious resistance, an elastic motion, which salt water has and fresh water has not. There is about them a wide wholesome air, full of vivid light and constant wind, which is only felt at sea. Life undulates and death palpitates in the splendid verse which resumes the evidence of a brave and clear-sighted man concerning life and death. Here, as at sea, there is enough and too much of fluctuation and intermission; the ripple flags and falls in loose and lazy lines: the foam flies wide of any mark, and the breakers collapse here and there in sudden ruin and violent failure. But the violence and weakness of the sea are preferable to the smooth sound and equable security of a lake: its buoyant and progressive impulse sustains and propels those who would sink through weariness in the flat and placid shallows. There are others whom it sickens, and others whom it chills; these will do well to steer inshore. . . .

Nothing in Byron is so worthy of wonder and admiration as the scope and range of his power. New fields and ways of work, had he lived, might have given room for exercise and matter for triumph to "that most fiery spirit." As it is, his work was done at Missolonghi; all of his work for which the fates could spare him time. A little space was allowed him to show at least a heroic purpose, to attest a high design; then, with all things unfinished before him and behind, he fell asleep after many troubles and triumphs. Few can ever have gone wearier to the grave; none with less fear. He had done enough to earn his rest. Forgetful now and set free for ever from all faults and foes, he passed through the doorway of no ignoble death out of reach of time, out of sight of love, out of hearing of hatred, beyond the blame of England and the praise of Greece. In the full strength of spirit and of body his destiny overtook him, and made an end of all his labours. He had seen and borne and achieved more than most men on record. "He was a great man, good at many things, and now he has attained this also, to be at rest."

NOTES

THE TRIUMPH OF TIME

In 1862 Swinburne met a 'graceful and vivacious' girl with whom he fell deeply in love. He believed that she had encouraged him—possibly because he was anxious to believe it—but when he declared his passion she merely laughed. Swinburne was possibly a little ridiculous and violent over his proposal, and the laughter may have been due more to nervousness than to unkindness, but he retired, deeply hurt and unhappy, to Northumberland. There he wrote this poem and "A Leave-Taking," each among the few really sincere of his love-poems, although "The Triumph of Time," like so much of his best work, is spoilt by its great length. Swinburne never again fell seriously in love.

35. *the great third wave*: the wave which is believed to be greater than its fellows is variously described as the ninth, the tenth, or the third. Burke has "the victorious tenth wave shall ride, like the boar, over all the rest" while Tennyson makes it the ninth. Cf. also Masefield, "Salt Water Ballads,"

> Send me a ninth great peaceful wave.

Swinburne, as an enthusiastic swimmer, must many a time have crossed and climbed a 'great third wave.'

ITYLUS

Tereus, King of Thrace, was married to Procne, who after a time grew anxious to see again her sister, Philomela. So Tereus went to Athens to fetch her, but on the way home he ill-treated her, and then cut out her tongue lest she should tell of her wrongs. He told his wife, Procne, that Philomela had died. But Philomela found her way to a cottage in Hellas, where she wove, in a robe that she sent to Procne, the story of her shame. Procne exacted a terrible revenge. She cooked their own son, Itylus, and served him up to Tereus, at Daulis, in a dish. As soon as the king discovered the truth he set out in pursuit of his wife, who had fled to Philomela.

The two princesses, fleeing in terror, prayed to the gods for help, whereupon Tereus was changed to a hawk, Procne to a swallow, and Philomela to a nightingale.

Here Swinburne imagines Philomela mourning for Itylus (the ancients found the song of the nightingale infinitely sad) and a little indignant that Procne can so readily find joy in the Spring and the South.

17. *tawny*: cf. Matthew Arnold, *Philomela*: "the tawny-throated." Arnold's poem should be read as a companion to "Itylus." Cf. also the "brown bright nightingale" in the "Hounds of Spring" chorus, p. 74.

29, 30. *Till life forget*, etc.: i.e. until life shall be the same thing as oblivion, and death the same as remembrance; that is, of course, never.

IN MEMORY OF WALTER SAVAGE LANDOR

In 1864 Swinburne was in Florence (he is said to have written "Itylus" in a garden filled with the music of noonday nightingales at Fiesole) and called upon Landor, then in his ninetieth year. His first visit was so tempestuous—he flung himself with so much vigour at the feet of the master—that it was not a success. He wrote for another interview, and this time, in a calmer spirit of adoration, was very kindly received. The old man was dead before the year was out. He is best known for his *Imaginary Conversations*, but had long been one of Swinburne's heroes, mainly because of his *Hellenics*.

1. *the flower-town*: Florence. Cf. Landor's Idyll beginning

Here, where precipitate Spring....

THE GARDEN OF PROSERPINE

Proserpine was wife of Pluto and queen of the Infernal Regions. In later legend, and mainly in Swinburne, she was Goddess of Sleep. Cf. Swinburne's "Hymn to Proserpine":

Thou art more than the day or the morrow, the seasons that laugh or that weep;
For these give joy and sorrow; but thou, Proserpina, sleep.

6, 7. *For reaping folk*, etc.: an example of the false antithesis referred to in the Introduction, p. x. The balance, *in sound*, is perfect, but not *in sense*, since 'mowing' does not bear the same relation to 'harvest-time' as 'sowing' bears to 'reaping-folk.'

41–44. This must not be taken too literally as an expression of Swinburne's faith—or lack of it. The poem was written, as the last stanza but one reveals, in a fit of reaction from his rather hectic life in London.

DEDICATION

To Edward Burne-Jones, a friend and fellow-worker of Swinburne, four years his senior. The dedication was placed, according to the poet's custom, at the end of the volume. The metre is that of "Dolores," and the poem is amazingly typical of Swinburne's versification. Note the alliterations, the slightly forced rhymes, and particularly the music of the verse, which tends to lull the critical faculties into accepting almost anything without question. It was this lilt that laid Swinburne open to facile parody.

27, 28. *Faustine*, etc.: characters, all more or less imaginary, to whom many of the most passionate poems were addressed.

45–48. Inaccurate. Swinburne himself has stated elsewhere that he destroyed every line he had written before the age of eighteen. It is interesting to note that Pope also, in after-life, pretended to have written some of his verses at a ridiculously early age. Pope's inaccuracy, however, was more dishonest and petty than Swinburne's, which Mr Gosse calls an "innocent mystification." He adds that about 1865 Swinburne "contrived to persuade himself, and to convince some of his friends, that he was three years younger than he really was. . .thereby laying many traps for posterity."

AVE ATQUE VALE

Written in April, 1867, when Swinburne was suffering from the shock of the news of the death of Baudelaire. The news proved false, although Baudelaire died a few months later. He was one of Swinburne's earliest heroes and the influence of his poetry can be seen in the earlier *Poems and Ballads*.

13. *gardener of strange flowers*: the title of Baudelaire's most famous book is *Les Fleurs du Mal*.

47. *this shut scroll*: the mere body, or perhaps Baudelaire's poems. The poet imagines himself beside the bier, standing beneath "veiled porches of a Muse funereal."

56. *sacred staff*: a reference to the Tannhauser legend. Tannhauser, having spent a year in the Venusberg with Venus, went to the Pope for absolution. "You can no more hope for mercy," said the Pope, "than this dry staff can be expected to bud again."

Tannhauser departed in despair, but three days later the staff burst into blossom. Tannhauser, meanwhile, had returned to Venus and could nowhere be found.

82. *Niobean womb*: Niobe was the mother of twelve children, all of whom were slain. (Cf. *Hamlet*: "Like Niobe, all tears.")

THE ARMADA

Swinburne's lines on the Armada were inflamed with a foolish and unworthy hatred of Roman Catholicism, a passion that jars and spoils the mighty sweep of the poem, with its beating internal rhymes and its long organ-roll of stanza. The more violent of these objectionable passages have been omitted from this selection.

4. *galleon and galliass*: the latter was not peculiarly a Spanish vessel as was the galleon. They were both descended, by different paths, from the Roman galley.

9. *bastions of serpentine*: serpentine is a rock of a certain silky lustre, found near the Lizard in Cornwall.

11. *bale*: calamity. Almost extinct except in 'baleful.'

81. *stinted of gear*: the shortage of ammunition was not due, as is so often suggested, to the parsimony of Queen Elizabeth so much as to the enormous and unprecedented speed with which it was used in the earlier stages of the battle. The Battle of the Armada marks, indeed, the beginning of a new age in naval warfare.

148. *Oquendo*: a Spanish admiral. He was by no means the only Spaniard to put up a gallant fight. See the *Cambridge Modern History* (vol. III) for an account of the battle.

170. *Catholic isle*: Ireland. There are legends, supported to some extent by the survival of Spanish types and names, that some ships of the Armada were wrecked off the Isle of Man, South Wales and Cornwall. In the Isle of Man there is even a 'Spanish Head' rock.

TO A SEAMEW

"The wistfulness of his later life whispers for a moment behind the back of Walter Watts." (Harold Nicolson.) Note particularly the regret in stanza x, ll. 75, 76, and cf. also the closing lines of "A Vision of Spring in Winter" (*Poems and Ballads, II*):

> But flowers thou may'st, and winds, and hours of ease,
> And all its April to the world thou may'st
> Give back, and half my April back to me.

THE BRIDE'S TRAGEDY

12. *My weird is ill to dree*: to 'dree one's weird' is to submit to one's lot. 'Weird' is here a noun, from the A.-S. *weorthan*, to be, and the adjective, 'weird,' originally meaning 'connected with, or influencing, fate' has lost its force. Sir J. M. Barrie has an amusing play with 'dreeing one's weird' in *Alice Sit-by-the-fire*.

24. *wyte*: blame.

29. *may*: maiden, possibly because May is the Spring-month.

47. *Chollerford*: on the North Tyne and near the Roman Wall.

50. *lift*: the sky.

53. *scathe*: injury.

A JACOBITE'S EXILE

16. *Drumossie*: the Battle of Culloden Moor, 1746.

25. *mool*: mould.

47. *thole*: suffer.

THALASSIUS

The last lines of a long poem which is, in a sense, autobiographical. It tells of a child, the son of the Sun-God, Apollo, and the Sea, who is abandoned on a desolate shore and there found by an imaginary being (i.e. the spirit common to Hugo, Mazzini, Landor, etc.), who tends him and teaches him the love of liberty, the hatred of oppression and all the other Swinburnian ideals. The boy sets out alone and meets Love, who appears at first a silent and harmless child, but whose eyes suddenly become hard and mocking

> And all his stature waxed immeasurable,
> As of one shadowing heaven;

and Love cries aloud

> O fool, my name is sorrow,
> Thou fool, my name is death,

and vanishes. Dancing and riot follow, until the pilgrim becomes sated and turns to the sea for purification; he regains the whiteness and purity of his childhood, and one day hears the voice of Apollo, his father,

> The old great voice of the old good time,

speaking to him, and feels his father's hand on his head.

PRELUDE

Compare this with the story of Thalassius and its conclusion. Swinburne appears to turn his back on the 'roses and raptures' of earlier days and to dedicate his future to high ideals. The abiding element, common to these new ideas and the old, is the sea, though slightly different in all that it stands for from the 'mother and lover of men' of his youth. The *Songs before Sunrise*, to which these stanzas were the prelude, do not all live up to the high ideals sketched here; the poet often "loses control," as Mr Nicolson says, "after the first two stanzas.....the reader's emotions are not engaged."

82. *To flush with love and hide in flowers*: possibly an allusion to *The Earthly Paradise*, published in 1868–70, in which William Morris proclaimed himself "the idle singer of an empty day."

TO WALT WHITMAN IN AMERICA

It is interesting to note that Swinburne, among the first to hail Whitman as a prophet of liberty, repudiated him in strong terms in 1887—a change which many attribute to the influence of Watts-Dunton, who was never able to see the merit of Whitman's work. In *Whitmania* Swinburne described the Muse of Whitman as "a drunken apple-woman, sprawling in the slush and garbage of the gutter, amid the rotten refuse of her over-turned fruit-stall."

29, 31. *clarion...carrion*: the same rhyme occurs again in "Mater Triumphalis." See Introduction, p. x.

90, 91. *How shall we sing*, etc.: for Swinburne's Biblical allusions see also the closing lines of "Song," p. 25.

MATER TRIUMPHALIS

Addressed to Liberty, the 'Mother Triumphant.' It is almost pathetic to compare the spirit that fired these stanzas with the actuality—Swinburne's passionate enthusiasm with his empty and restricted life at Putney.

61, 62. *The crowned heads*, etc.: perhaps a reference to the victories already won against Austria in Italy.

COR CORDIUM

Addressed to Shelley.

PERINDE AC CADAVER

England was by no means so aloof and unsympathetic as Swinburne implies. Mazzini lived many years here an exile, and, later, Garibaldi was given a splendid reception. It would have been impossible, in the nature of things, for England to have 'taken sides' very definitely, and Swinburne knew this. It is important to remember that he was a stern lover of England, and fiercely resented any criticism of Queen Victoria. See the opening stanzas of "The Commonweal, 1887" (not in this selection).

16. *the goddess*: i.e. Liberty.

THE OBLATION

From its inclusion in *Songs before Sunrise* this poem must be taken as a restatement of Swinburne's dedication of himself to the great Cause; it is equally capable of a more personal interpretation.

ATALANTA IN CALYDON

FIRST CHORUS

6, 7, 8. *Itylus, Thracian ships, tongueless vigil*: see p. 111 for the story of Itylus.

22. *harp-player*: note the accent on the last syllable of 'player'—a trick common to the pre-Raphaelite poets.

38. *the oat*: i.e. the shepherd's oaten stem, used as a musical pipe.

44. *Maenad, Bassarid*: bacchantes, revellers.

49. *Bacchanal*: a priestess of Bacchus; they wore fillets of ivy in the hair.

ALTHÆA'S SPEECH

Compare this brief description of a storm (ll. 9–11) with the longer description in *Tristram*, p. 71.

'This man,' in the first line, is Meleager.

MELEAGER TO ALTHÆA

29. *irremeable*: permitting of no return. (Lat. *meo*, to go; not connected with *remus*, an oar.)

Symplegades: the Cyanean rocks at the entrance to the Euxine. They were said to dash together when a vessel attempted to pass through, but the Argonauts, having sent a dove through (which lost only the tip of its tail) slipped through immediately, almost without damage.

31. *Colchis*: the island of Æetes and the Golden Fleece.

46. It was with the aid of Medea that Jason was able to perform the various feats imposed by Æetes, and so secure the Fleece.

LAST CHORUS

20. *a blast of the envy of God*: Frank Harris says of this line: "What did it matter to us that this phrase was taken from Euripides? It had a new weight in English, an added value."

Note. In the Greek, Meleager is married to a wife, Cleopatra, who tends him in his last moments. Swinburne, in his version, omits her and makes Meleager insensible to the charms of women until he meets the fresh and virginal Atalanta.

ADIEUX À MARIE STUART

Written on the completion of *Mary Stuart* (1881), the last of Swinburne's great trilogy around the central figure of Mary Queen of Scots.

1. *my fathers fought*: this was more than a justifiable hazard on Swinburne's part. There was a family legend that an ancestor, Thomas Swinburne of Capheaton, took arms for the defence of Mary Stuart and fell, like most men who came into contact with her, a slave to her beauty.

24. *Hermitage*: thirty years earlier, Swinburne had made a pilgrimage to Roxburghshire, where, on the banks of the Water of Hermitage, Mary Stuart was said to have made a visit to Bothwell, who lay there in a small fort, wounded. It is to this visit of his youth that the poet refers.

NEPHELIDIA

From *The Heptalogia, or the Seven Against Sense* (cf. Aeschylus, *The Seven Against Thebes*), in which Swinburne parodies seven poets, including himself. It is often said that Swinburne lacked a sense of humour, but "Nephelidia," if it does not actually disprove the statement, shows at least that he was aware of his own peculiarities and of the extent to which they lent themselves to exaggeration and parody. The title, in so far as it means anything, means "Cloudiness." "Nepheliads" are cloud nymphs.

A SWIMMER'S DREAM

23, 24. *here too soon*, etc.: the wistful note again. Notice how, as in "To a Seamew," the poet likens himself to a sea-bird—each time a little regretfully—although he is, for the rest of this poem, a swimmer!

ETON: AN ODE

3. *a wise man*: Henry VI.
22. *Still the reaches*, etc.: these three lines were inscribed on a wreath sent from Eton to Swinburne's funeral.

A CHANNEL PASSAGE

The record of an actual storm experienced during a crossing from Ostend when the poet was eighteen. The word 'Calais' in the first line is a slip of memory. The crossing took place in 1855, and the poem was published in 1904 and written, probably, shortly before that date.

21. *shores where never was man born free*: Swinburne is unable to keep away from his obsession even at the age of seventy, in a descriptive 'nature-poem,' one of the few essentially descriptive pieces he wrote.

REVIEW OF *L'HOMME QUI RIT*

Compare this prose passage with the verse description in "A Channel Passage." This passage was written more than thirty years before the poem, but apart from the more definite recollection, in the poet's memory, of the storm there is also noticeable a more definite style and a crisper description in the prose passage. Not all Swinburne's prose was as clear and forcible as this.

Oceanides: nymphs of the Ocean. (In biology, marine mollusca, as distinguished from Naiades, or 'Fresh-water Shells.')

Artemis: Greek name of Diana, Goddess of light, etc.

Titans: the giants (said to be the children of Heaven and Earth) who had warred against Zeus, been defeated, and thrown into Tartarus.

BYRON

Written for an introduction to a selection of Byron's poems; the last paragraph is generally reckoned to be the finest piece of prose that Swinburne ever wrote, but note, even here, the insistence on alliteration, as in "forgetful now and set free for ever from all faults and foes."

Byron was another of the earlier idols whom Swinburne afterwards repudiated.

that most fiery spirit: from Shelley's *Lines written on hearing the news of the Death of Napoleon.*

Missolonghi: where Byron died, in 1824, having joined the Greek forces in their War of Independence.

For EU product safety concerns, contact us at Calle de José Abascal, 56–1°, 28003 Madrid, Spain or eugpsr@cambridge.org.

www.ingramcontent.com/pod-product-compliance
Ingram Content Group UK Ltd.
Pitfield, Milton Keynes, MK11 3LW, UK
UKHW012333130625
459647UK00009B/248

* 9 7 8 1 1 0 7 6 8 1 6 2 0 *